Equitable Access for English Learners

Grades K-6

We dedicate this book to those creative teachers who provide equitable access to all their students, including their English learners, as they teach their language arts curriculum.

Equitable Access for English Learners

Grades K-6

Strategies and Units for Differentiating Your Language Arts Curriculum

Mary Soto, David E. Freeman,
and Yvonne S. Freeman

A SAGE Publishing Company

FOR INFORMATION:

Corwin
A SAGE Company
2455 Teller Road
Thousand Oaks, California 91320
(800) 233-9936
www.corwin.com

SAGE Publications Ltd.
1 Oliver's Yard
55 City Road
London, EC1Y 1SP
United Kingdom

SAGE Publications India Pvt. Ltd.
B 1/I 1 Mohan Cooperative Industrial Area
Mathura Road, New Delhi 110 044
India

SAGE Publications Asia-Pacific Pte. Ltd.
18 Cross Street #10-10/11/12
China Square Central
Singapore 048423

Program Director and Publisher: Dan Alpert
Content Development Editor: Lucas Schleicher
Senior Editorial Assistant: Mia Rodriguez
Production Editor: Tori Mirsadjadi
Copy Editor: Paula Bonilla
Typesetter: Hurix Digital
Proofreader: Lawrence W. Baker
Indexer: Mary Mortensen
Cover Designer: Rose Storey
Marketing Manager: Sharon Pendergast

This book is printed on acid-free paper.

20 21 22 23 24 10 9 8 7 6 5 4 3 2 1

Contents

Visit the companion website at **resources.corwin.com/ EquitableAccessK6** for downloadable resources.

Acknowledgments

We wish to acknowledge the efforts of the team at Corwin who have supported the development of this book. Maura Sullivan is a long-time colleague who has encouraged us as we have written many of our books. Presently, Maura is the director of marketing strategy and business development at Corwin. She has been actively involved in the production of *Equitable Access* from its inception.

Dan Alpert, our editor, provided insightful advice that helped shape our manuscript. His expertise in and understanding of language acquisition and his commitment to providing equitable education for all students were invaluable as we wrote and revised this book.

We also want to acknowledge the careful attention to detail that Mia Rodriguez, senior editorial assistant, and Lucas Schleicher, content development editor, gave to the production of the book. They worked on the layout and figures as well as developing the companion website with blackline masters to ensure a final high quality and reader-friendly product. Paula Bonilla provided the careful copyediting that is crucial for any book. Tori Mirsadjadi, project editor, oversaw all the steps involved in producing this book.

Ann Ebe, a knowledgeable teacher educator, provided many of the the the photos and ideas for the seed unit that we describe in Chapter Two of Part Two of this book.

This book brings together what we have learned from students in schools, graduate students, and fellow university professors and researchers in the fields of ESL and bilingual education and literacy. We acknowledge the influence of all of these dedicated educators to this book.

Publisher's Acknowledgments

Corwin gratefully acknowledges the contributions of the following reviewers:

Natalie Bernasconi
English Teacher, University Instructor
Salinas Union High School District, UC Santa Cruz
Santa Cruz, CA

Stacey Lemongelli, NBCT
District Instructional Leader, ELA
Perth Amboy Public School Districts
Amboy, NJ

Courtney Pawol
First Grade Teacher
Portland Public Schools
Portland, OR

Gloria Pennell
Retired Educator
Bergenfield High School
Bergenfield, NJ

Judith Quon
Teacher
Apple Valley Unified School District
Apple Valley, CA

Barbara Smith
Reading Teacher
Mattituck Cutchogue UFSD
Cutchogue, NY

About the Authors

Mary Soto, an assistant professor in the teacher education department at California State University East Bay, prepares teacher candidates and masters students to work with diverse learners. She is a coauthor of *ESL Teaching: Principles for Success* (Heinemann, 2016) and has published articles on the topic of bilingual/ESL teaching. She presents at national and international conferences. Her research interests focus on best practices for long-term English Learners.

Dr. David E. Freeman and **Dr. Yvonne S. Freeman** are professors emeriti at the University of Texas Rio Grande Valley. Both are interested in effective education for emergent bilinguals. They present regularly at international, national, and state conferences. They have worked extensively in schools in the United States. They have also worked with educators in Ecuador, Mexico, Colombia, Venezuela, Costa Rica, Argentina, Uruguay, Hong Kong, India, Indonesia, Lithuania, Mallorca, and Sweden.

The Freemans have authored books, articles, and book chapters jointly and separately on the topics of second language teaching, biliteracy, bilingual education, linguistics, and second language acquisition. They are authors of *Grammar and Syntax in Context* published by Corwin. Their books published by Heinemann include *Dual Language Essentials for Teachers and Administrators*, 2nd edition; *ESL Teaching: Principles for Success*, 2nd edition; *Essential Linguistics: What Teachers Need to Know to Teach ESL, Reading, Spelling, and Grammar*, 2nd edition; *Between Worlds: Access to Second Language Acquisition*, 3rd edition; *Academic Language for English Language Learners and Struggling Readers; La enseñanza de la lectura y la escritura en español y en inglés en clases bilingües y de doble inmersión*, 2nd edition; *Teaching Reading and Writing in Spanish and English in Bilingual and Dual Language Classrooms*, 2nd edition; *Closing the Achievement Gap: How to Reach Limited Formal Schooling and Long-Term English Learners*, and *Teaching Reading in Multilingual Classrooms*.

In addition, the Freemans have edited three books: *Research on Preparing Inservice Teachers to Work Effectively with Emergent Bilinguals* and *Research on Preparing Preservice Teachers to Work Effectively with Emergent Bilinguals* (Emerald Publishing), and *Diverse Learners in the Mainstream Classroom: Strategies for Supporting All Students Across Content Areas* (Heinemann).

PART ONE

The Equitable Access Approach

As the number of English learners in schools across the country increases, more and more mainstream teachers are teaching in classes that include both native English speakers and English learners. These teachers are expected to help all their students meet rigorous college and career readiness Standards using a language arts curriculum designed for native English speakers. To meet the demands now placed on teachers, we have designed the Equitable Access Approach (EAA) for English learners. This approach is not simply an add-on for English learners. Rather it is a way of teaching that can help the diverse students in language arts classrooms meet the challenge of the Standards and become successful readers and writers.

English learners are also referred to as emergent bilinguals (EBs), English language learners (ELLs), multilingual language learners (MLLs), and second language learners. We will use different terms throughout the book; however, the term we prefer is *emergent bilinguals* because this term emphasizes that as these students learn English, they are becoming bilingual and that being bilingual is an asset.

In this book, we present foundational concepts that help teachers support English learners as they read, write about, and discuss their language arts curriculum. We demonstrate how these concepts are put into practice by describing in detail four commonly taught English language arts units. The units we describe show how teachers in mainstream classes can differentiate their language arts curriculum to make it accessible to all their students, including their emergent bilinguals.

We encourage teachers to read and discuss this book in pairs or groups, preferably with colleagues teaching in the same school or district. However, this book is meant for individual teachers as well.

When reflection activities are suggested, we encourage all readers to consider the reflections. If there are not others to talk with, readers might jot down thoughts to come back to as they continue through the book and try out the strategies suggested.

In this Part One section, we introduce the Equitable Access Approach and encourage readers to think about, analyze, and talk about their language arts reading programs. In Part Two, we present the units through a description of how four teachers, two lower elementary and two upper elementary, give equitable access to their language arts curriculum and draw upon key concepts that support all students, especially English learners. The teachers we describe all follow important practices for teaching emergent bilinguals as they teach the units. At the beginning of each chapter, we present a key concept teachers can apply as they teach emergent bilingual students. Next, as we describe the activities in the unit, we show how the teacher implements the key concept.

In Part Two, Chapter Two, "Language Objectives: A Seeds, Plants, and Plant Growth Unit," we introduce how teachers write and implement language objectives to help students meet the academic content objectives required in the Standards. In Part Two, Chapter Three, "Making the Input Comprehensible: A Habitats Unit," we provide specific ways teachers can make their instructional input comprehensible, including how teachers can draw on their students' first languages even when the teachers themselves don't speak them. In Chapter Four, "Characteristics of Texts That Support Readers: Our Amazing Oceans Unit," we provide a list of the characteristics of texts that support readers and a rubric that helps teachers determine the cultural relevance of texts for their students. In the final chapter, Chapter Five, "Teaching Academic Language and Meaningful Content: Our Earth, Natural Disasters Unit," we explain how teachers can help students develop academic content knowledge and develop greater academic language proficiency in the context of a unit on natural disasters.

When teachers adopt the Equitable Access Approach, which is designed to help all students meet the Standards, their emergent bilinguals succeed, and they find the language arts curriculum more meaningful and engaging. At the same time, teachers get to know their students so that they can better meet their needs. They draw on their students' language and cultural resources to enrich classroom discussions and activities. They approach reading in meaningful ways by supporting them and then gradually releasing the responsibility for reading to the reader. Through engaging students actively, they help them develop both academic English and content knowledge.

Why This Book?

This book is intended to meet the needs of novice and experienced teachers across the country who are required to use language arts materials designed for native English speakers in classrooms with students at different levels of English proficiency. While students with limited English proficiency may be provided with help from an English as a second language (ESL) teacher, in most cases mainstream teachers teach both native English speakers and students whose home language is not English in the same class. Throughout this book, we provide teachers with practical and easy strategies they can use to provide equitable access for all students to the language arts curriculum.

Basals and supplemental language arts programs usually list a few additional ideas for teachers to use to support English learners (ELs) in their classes. However, the strategies we describe are not intended as add-ons for ELs. Instead, taken together, they constitute an approach that works effectively for all students. When teachers use this approach as they teach the units in their language arts program, all their students have equitable access to the academic content.

Required readings that are connected to Standards based units of study must be accessible to students who are not fully proficient in English. And ELs must be able to read, write about, and discuss these readings. For that reason, for each unit we identify specific, Standards based skills that students develop as they engage in the activity. We also list genres students develop during some activities that require them to write specific genres, such as letter writing or poetry.

In the first chapter, we engage readers in thinking about, analyzing, and discussing their language arts reading programs. We also discuss the importance of teaching emergent bilinguals through units of inquiry. The units of inquiry include activities that enable teachers to learn about their students, to create a multilingual, multicultural environment, to assess their students' language proficiency, to use a gradual release model for reading and writing, to draw on students' backgrounds and cultures, and to draw on students' home languages by using translanguaging strategies.

Many of the activities to help readers reflect on their language arts programs that we describe in this chapter can also be applied while teaching a unit of study during language arts. So, for example, a variation on the following teacher reflection activities can be applied to analysis of characters in a story in the language arts program.

Positive/Negative Graph

On the graph that follows (Figure 0.1), place a letter (A–G) to evaluate how appropriate each of the components of your language arts materials is for your English learners. For example, if you feel that the Teacher's Edition includes good suggestions for making the lessons accessible for English learners, you might place the letter A by +4 or +5 on the graph. Or if you believe the reading selections are too difficult for your English learners, place the letter B by –4 or –5.

I. COMPONENTS

A. Teacher's Edition

B. Reading selections

C. Phonics instruction

D. Comprehension activities

E. Workbooks

F. Assessments

G. Writing activities

Figure 0.1   Positive/Negative Graph

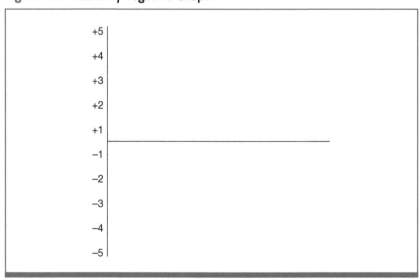

- Standards based skills: *create, infer/predict, evaluate, recall, explain, compare and contrast*

2. TURN AND TALK

Turn and talk with a partner about your graphs. Where did you place each of your letters on the graph? Why? Do you ever worry about whether all your students understand the stories and activities in your language arts program? Do you think the students understand what they are reading? Do they have experiences that help them read, write about, and discuss the reading selections? Do the activities supplied in the program materials help English learners access the content?

- Standards based skills: *create, infer/predict, evaluate, recall, explain, compare and contrast*

- Classroom applications of positive/negative graph:

  1. *Students list positive and negative events in their life. The vertical axis is numbered 1–5 to show how positive or negative the event was, and the horizontal axis reflects student's age. Students use this graph to write an autobiographical essay.*

  2. *As applied to a novel, the horizontal axis could indicate events in a chapter or events in a character's life. These would be rated 1–5 to show how positive or negative the event was.*

  3. *As applied to a text recounting history, the horizontal line could be a timeline and then events could be rated positive through negative along the timeline.*

CHAPTER ONE

Foundations for the Equitable Access Approach for English Learners

MANDATED LANGUAGE ARTS PROGRAMS

Across the country, teachers are faced with the challenge of teaching multilingual, multicultural learners following state and district Standards. Elementary language arts teachers, in particular, are required to meet Standards that are aligned with standardized tests used to measure school and teacher effectiveness. School district administrators, pressured by their local communities to have exemplary schools, look for materials and programs that guarantee success.

Publishers have responded to these demands by producing language arts materials that claim to meet state Standards and claim to include everything teachers need to ensure that all their students will succeed when evaluated. Most programs used in schools are referred to as basal readers or core reading programs and are meant to provide a sequenced approach to reading instruction through textbooks and supplemental materials that include readings (often excerpts from children's literature) and skills instruction.

Basal programs regularly include claims that they have research evidence showing their programs promote the success of all students. However, several studies have brought these claims into question.

With the adoption of the Common Core State Standards (CCSS), expectations for all students, including emergent bilinguals, are much higher.

As Fu and her colleagues point out, the new Standards "put pressure on EB's [emergent bilinguals] capabilities and prove more taxing for their long-term success" (Fu, Hadjioannou, & Zhou, 2019, p. 22). In California and New York, the two states with the highest numbers of English learners, only 25% and 29% of ELs met grade-level expectations. Further, "Emergent bilingual students scored markedly worse on the California Standardized Test where, in the 2nd grade, there was a 20% disparity between EBs and their English proficient counterparts (45% EB versus 64% English proficient passing rate)" (Fu, Hadjioannou, & Zhou, 2019, p. 22).

Although basal programs claim they contain all the components needed for every student to succeed, in his article "The Problem With Literacy Programs," published in *Education Week,* Schmoker states:

> We must reckon with the fact that even popular, highly praised commercial programs often lack a robust evidence base. That's because they are deficient in precisely those aspects most critical to acquiring the ability to read, write, and speak well. Instead, they abound in busywork. (p. 18)

Schmoker points out that while programs may be well-designed, they are often poorly implemented and do not provide time for students to read, write, and discuss text. Rather, they engage students in many worksheets both on paper and in electronic form.

Several companies have developed programs that are alternatives to basal programs. These alternative comprehensive literacy programs are usually developed following key shifts in curriculum and instruction. They are designed to meet the rigor and expectations of the new Standards and are meant to be more meaningful for students. However, it is difficult for any program to be appropriate for all students.

In 2010, Education Market Research reported that 74% of classroom teachers used district- or school-adopted basal reading programs (Dewitz & Jones, 2012). This percentage of teachers using basal reading programs published by major publishing companies such as Houghton Mifflin Harcourt and Macmillan/McGraw-Hill has remained at around 70% for a number of years. The remaining districts or schools either adopt alternative literacy programs that also are considered comprehensive literacy programs or work with their teachers using authentic literature and develop their own units connected to Standards.

Using basal programs has pros and cons. They are chosen for a variety of reasons (Dewitz, Leahy, & Jones, 2010; Y. Freeman, 1988a; Goodman, Shannon, Freeman, & Murphy, 1988; Shanahan, 2016):

Pros

- Basal programs support novice teachers by including units, supplemental materials, and lesson plans.
- Basals provide lesson plans, so teachers need less planning time.
- Basals include assessments for monitoring progress.
- Basals include worksheets and many activities teachers can draw upon.
- Basals promise to provide administrators and reading directors evidence that important reading skills are being taught in a systematic way.

Over the years, however, basal reading programs have been analyzed and critiqued. Research has suggested that basal programs have several problems (Chambliss & Calfee, 1998; Dewitz, Jones, & Leahy, 2009; Dewitz et al., 2010; D. E. Freeman & Y. Freeman, 1999; Y. Freeman, 1988a, 1988b; Goodman et al., 1988; McKeown, Beck, & Blake, 2009; Walsh, 2003):

Cons

- Basal programs respond to education trends and are market driven but rarely initiate new ideas and rarely reflect reading research.
- Programs are developed by editors, graphic designers, and marketing experts who give prototypical lesson plans to companies that specialize in writing the materials.
- Despite publisher claims, basal programs are more alike than they are different.

- Materials in the programs include repetitive questions and activities that bore students.
- Basal programs are developed for groups of students, not individual students who have distinct needs.
- Basal programs do not reflect a variety of teaching methods for different types of students.
- Basal programs fail to draw on background knowledge of diverse students.
- Basal materials do not take into account students' varied academic strengths and abilities or English proficiency.

Take a few minutes to review and reflect on the following summary chart of the pros and cons of basal programs.

Figure 1.1   What Research Says About Basal Reading Programs

PROS	CONS
Program materials give guidance to novice teachers.	Programs reflect market needs and trends, not research.
Programs save teachers planning time.	Programs are not written by reading experts.
Programs include assessment of progress.	Programs are more alike than different.
Programs include lots of materials for teachers to use.	Programs include boring, repetitive materials.
Programs assure administrators reading is being taught in a consistent way.	Programs do not support different student needs.
	Programs do not draw on students' background knowledge.
	Programs do not consider different academic abilities or the English proficiency of students.

1. TURN AND TALK

Do you agree with the pros and cons of using a basal reading program in your classroom? Which of the pros do you agree with? Which of the cons do you agree with and which of these are causing you the most concern? Do you have students who are lost most of the time you are teaching your language arts curriculum? Do you know why? With your partner, add to the pros and cons listed in Figure 1.1.

- <u>Standards based skills:</u> *draw on background knowledge, evaluate, recall, explain, compare and contrast, formulate opinion*

- <u>Classroom activities for pros and cons activity:</u>
  1. *This process could be applied to a persuasive essay or a debate topic.*

2. "WHAT IF . . . THEN" POEM

Write a "What if . . . Then" poem to complete the following prompt:

"What if I used a series of strategies to make my mandated language arts curriculum more comprehensible for my English learners?" The structure of the poem is as follows:

- *What if . . .*

- *Then . . .*

- *And . . .*

- *And . . .*

- *Share with your group.*

- <u>Standards based skills:</u> *predict/infer, evaluate, create*

- <u>Classroom activities for a What If . . . Then poem:</u>
  1. *This activity could be used to imagine how events in a story would have changed if one event had been different.*
  2. *The activity can also apply to a historical text.*

Support for English Learners in Basals

In the process of developing this book, we performed our own analysis of widely used basal series. This analysis informed the conclusions of the following subsections of this chapter.

Basal programs and alternative programs include instructions for teaching the lessons to emergent bilinguals. Some suggestions for ELs are typically included in a given program's teacher's guide as part of the instructions for each selection. However, teachers are often directed to look in another section of the guide for more detailed ideas for ELs. In addition, major basal programs provide suggestions for English learners in a separate resource book. To develop their lessons, then, teachers have to consult two sections of the teacher's guide plus a separate document.

SUPPORT INSTRUCTION IN THE TEACHER'S GUIDE

Most suggestions included in the teacher's guides to basal programs focus on direct instruction of vocabulary. Key words for each selection are pre-taught. Many programs include vocabulary cards, another resource that teachers must search for within the program materials and have ready to use. The cards usually include drawings to help students understand each word and a sample sentence using the word. Teachers are instructed to define the word and show the picture. It should be noted that the pictures and their relation to the words are not always clear, even to native English speakers. Often, the instructions direct teachers to have the ELs repeat the word two or three times. Students might also be asked to explain the word to a partner. This practice of pre-teaching vocabulary words is almost always the first suggestion for supporting English learners, despite research (Anderson & Nagy, 1992) showing that vocabulary is more readily acquired in the context of reading rather than by studying isolated words out of context.

Another common suggestion for working with ELs is to have the students repeat after the teacher. For example, students might be asked to repeat the selection title or the author's name as well as key words from the reading selection. Another repetition activity also promoted is echo reading. In echo reading, the teacher reads a short text section aloud, and English learners echo (repeat) what the teacher says. This practice is commonly used for emergent bilinguals at beginning and intermediate proficiency levels. While this activity can be useful at times, it should not be used with every lesson and should be tailored to a students' needs and levels of English proficiency. However, the basal supports for ELs typically don't differentiate by English proficiency levels.

An activity sometimes suggested for English learners is to distinguish between words that are minimal pairs. Minimal pairs are words that differ by one sound (or phoneme) such as *big* and *bag* or *big* and *pig*. Having students repeat minimal pairs or identify which word of a pair the teacher has pronounced is a practice that was commonly used in teaching ESL in the past. There is little purpose in repeating isolated words, usually not related to the readings in the lesson, and there is no research showing that this practice improves listening, speaking, or reading skills. An overarching goal for English learners in a basal program should be to build comprehension of academic English during reading: Activities such as identifying words from minimal pairs does not serve the interest of helping students improve their reading comprehension.

SEPARATE EL RESOURCE BOOK

Most basal programs include a resource book and online resources for emergent bilinguals. In a typical program, teachers are directed to have English learners listen to a recorded version of the text selection, usually provided as an online resource before the reading lesson. The teacher then pre-teaches key vocabulary from the reading. After that, the teacher follows a script to teach the selection. First, the teacher reads the text aloud, one paragraph or short section at a time, and then stops after each paragraph or section and asks a series of questions to guide students through the reading. This plan for supporting English learners is teacher centered rather than student centered and seldom engages students in meaningful language use. Further, there is no attempt to shift the responsibility from the teacher to the students. Instruction should help emergent bilinguals develop the skills needed to become independent readers.

Basal program teacher scripts are designed to present some background or context for the reading, define key vocabulary, and build understanding. Questions are often based on the pictures in the text. Teachers ask students about what they see in the picture. The resource guide provides teachers with expected answers from the students.

There are several problems to an approach that uses a question-answer script. Many of the questions teachers are supposed to ask are syntactically complex and contain vocabulary that many emergent bilinguals could not be expected to have acquired. Since language acquisition results from receiving comprehensible input, it is unlikely students would benefit from questions that are incomprehensible to them. Further, asking and answering questions is an oral exercise.

Although the development of oral English is important for learning to read, during reading instruction time students should spend most of their time interacting with written text.

The question-answer format follows a traditional IRE (initiation, response, evaluation) approach to teaching that has been shown to be ineffective in promoting either language development or content knowledge. It discourages real language-rich discussions and higher-order thinking because most questions have only one answer that is found in the story selection. Another problem is that stopping to ask questions after each paragraph breaks up the reading and makes text comprehension more difficult. This IRE approach is different from a gradual release of responsibility model with read alouds, shared reading, guided reading, and independent reading that focuses on comprehension of whole texts and moves students toward reading independence.

Finally, one of the major dilemmas facing nearly every teacher is not having sufficient time to meet instructional objectives. The underlying assumption of EL activities in basals is that teachers must take *extra* time to implement these activities with English learners, despite the fact that teachers in mainstream classes have only limited time for teaching language arts.

Rather than using supplemental activities to meet the needs of emergent bilinguals, teachers need an approach that can be effective for both English learners and native English speakers. In this book, we describe an approach teachers can use for all their students. The strategies we describe are designed to build background; help students develop language arts skills; and actively engage students in reading, writing, and discussing key concepts as they study different inquiry units in their language arts reading programs.

In the chapters that follow, we provide four sample units of inquiry commonly found in mandated English language arts programs. For each of these units, we suggest strategies that will effectively engage and support all students, including English learners. For each strategy, we suggest Standards based skills these activities help students develop. We also include content and language objectives for different activities in each unit. These sample units of inquiry provide examples of an approach that teachers can use in language arts instruction. At the end of each chapter, we summarize the strategies used throughout the unit. We also list additional texts teachers can use to supplement the unit.

KEY PRACTICES FOR WORKING WITH ENGLISH LEARNERS

In addition to explaining specific strategies, the units we describe exemplify several key practices for working with emergent bilinguals. These practices are essential to effective teaching. In the following sections, we briefly discuss each of the following key practices.

- Organizing around big question units of inquiry
- Getting to know your English learners so you can best teach them
- Creating a multilingual/multicultural environment
- Understanding the language proficiency of your students
- Using a gradual release of responsibility model of reading and writing
- Drawing on English learners' background knowledge and cultures
- Drawing on students' home languages using translanguaging strategies

Organizing Around Big Question Units of Inquiry

As you teach the units in your basal program, you will see that the publisher has chosen readings that are connected to a topic or theme, such as weather or animal habitats. One of the key ways to help English learners understand the readings and acquire needed skills and vocabulary is to help them see the relationships among the readings. You can do this by having the students answer an overarching question as they become involved in the unit. For example, you could ask, "How does the weather affect our lives?" While it is good to make the connections among the readings and activities salient for all your students by linking them to a big question, it is especially critical for students who are not yet proficient in English. There are several reasons you should organize your teaching around units of inquiry based on big questions:

1. Because students see the big picture, the English instruction is more comprehensible.
2. Content areas (math, science, social studies, language arts) are interrelated.
3. Vocabulary is repeated naturally, as it appears in different content area studies.
4. Because the curriculum makes sense, second language learners are more fully engaged and experience more success.

5. Teachers can differentiate instruction to accommodate differences in students' language proficiency.
6. Through inquiry units, teachers can connect curriculum to students' lives and backgrounds.

Collaborative Unit Brainstorming Activity

Sit in grade level groups with others who are using your same basal reading program. Choose a unit from your basal. Together, use a large piece of butcher paper to create a poster reflecting how you will approach organizing the unit of inquiry. Begin by deciding on the big question for the unit. Looking at the reasons for organizing around units of inquiry, include in your poster:

- *how you will bring in different content areas*

- *what vocabulary will be repeated naturally through the stories and activities*

- *how you can differentiate instruction*

- *how you will connect the readings and activities to your students' lives*

As you create your poster, you may want to use the graphic organizer that follows (Figure 1.2). Modify it to fit the categories you want to include.

Figure 1.2   Theme Graphic Organizer

Language Arts	**Science**
• Stories	• Readings
• Activities	• Activities
• Vocabulary	• Vocabulary
• Connection to students' lives	• Connection to students' lives
Big Question for the Unit	
Math	**Social Studies**
• Activities	• Readings
• Vocabulary	• Activities
• Connection to students' lives	• Vocabulary
	• Connection to students' lives

- <u>Standards based skills</u>: *draw on background knowledge, select, explain, create*

Getting to Know Your Students

There are significant differences among the students we refer to as English language learners. Some have arrived recently while others were born in the United States or have lived in the United States most of their lives. Some come with more formal schooling than others. And some have already learned some English, while others are just beginning to learn it. Although there are individual differences among emergent bilinguals in each group we describe below, it is helpful to begin by considering the major types of English learners.

Below is a chart of different types of English learners you might see in your elementary classroom (Figure 1.3). Read over the characteristics of each.

Figure 1.3   Types of English Learners

Newly arrived with adequate schooling	• recent arrivals (less than five years in the United States) • typically in grades 2–6 • adequate schooling in home country • literate in their home language • soon catch up academically • may still score low on standardized tests given in English • social and economic factors can influence positively or negatively
Newly arrived with limited formal schooling (may be referred to as SIFE students— students with interrupted formal education)	• recent arrivals (less than five years in the United States) • typically in grades 2–6 • interrupted or limited schooling in home country • limited home language literacy • below grade level in math • poor academic achievement • social and economic factors can influence positively or negatively
Long-term English learner	• six or more years in U.S. schools • typically in grades 4–6 • limited literacy in both home language and English • some may get adequate grades but score low on tests • struggle with content classes

	• often have been retained and are at risk of dropping out
	• are *vaivén* students (return to their country and come back, often several times) or students with inconsistent/subtractive schooling
	• have had ESL or bilingual instruction, but no consistent program
Potential long-term English learner	• students in grades K–3 who do not receive adequate ESL or bilingual support
	• parents with low levels of education
	• parents struggling financially and/or socially

1. TURN AND TALK (GROUPS OF FOUR OR MORE)

Each person in your group should focus on a type of learner. Identify one of your current or past students who fits this category. Share what you know about that student. What more would you like to know about that student? Do you know about the student's previous schooling and literacy in the first language?

- <u>Standards based skills:</u> *summarize, identify, evaluate, analyze*

2. FOUR CORNERS ACTIVITY

You each have a card to write on. In each corner of the room, there is a sheet of paper with the title of one of the four types of students listed above. Which of the types of students do you have or think you have in your classroom? List students' names and characteristics on your card. Then, go to the corner that represents the type of student you identified. Discuss with others in your corner. Report out to the rest of the group.

- <u>Standards based skills:</u> *analyze, evaluate, formulate opinions, support ideas with evidence*

- <u>Classroom activities for a Four Corners activity:</u>
  1. *To draw on background knowledge and to find out what students already know about key concepts they will be studying, choose four concepts or photos representing the concepts and divide students into four groups. Each group could meet to record what they know about the concept and then report back to the class.*
  2. *When studying a debatable topic, choose four possible responses to the debate (strongly agree, agree, disagree, strongly agree). Have students go to the corner that represents their opinion, talk together, and then present their argument to the class.*

Creating a Multilingual/Multicultural Environment

It is important to find out about your students' languages and cultural backgrounds early in the school year. You might have records that the school provides, but often student information is not available. In today's diverse classrooms, it is not unusual for students to represent a variety of cultures and languages. Different activities provide opportunities for getting to know your students and helping students to get to know one another. These activities also encourage oral language development and help teachers create a multilingual/multicultural environment in their classrooms. When charts, objects, and student work reflecting cultures and languages other than English are posted around the classroom, diversity is celebrated, and students of different cultural and linguistic backgrounds are validated. Teachers have found the following activities effective for getting to know their students and creating a multilingual/multicultural environment.

I. WHERE IN THE WORLD ARE YOU FROM? MAP.

This project is simple, teaches you about your students, and celebrates students' backgrounds. A world map is on a classroom wall with a picture of each student arranged around the map. Students are asked, "Where were you born?" They locate where they were born on the map. Next, they draw an arrow or take a piece of yarn and connect it from their birthplace to their picture. See Figure I.4 for an example. If most students were born in the United States, a second question, "Where were your parents (or grandparents) born?" could be added and students could use a different color of arrow or yarn to indicate where their parents come from. If students aren't sure, they could ask their parents or grandparents. Students share where they or their family members are from and classmates ask questions and make comments.

- Standards based skills: *oral language development, compare and contrast, map reading*

2. COUNTRY AND FLAG GRAPH.

Ask students where they were born. Research the correct flag for each country mentioned. Have students draw a flag of their country of origin or use an Internet image. Then use the flags to create a graph that shows the number of students in your classroom from each country represented. Students share their flags and where they are from. See Figure I.5 for an example.

Figure 1.4   Where in the World Are You From? Map

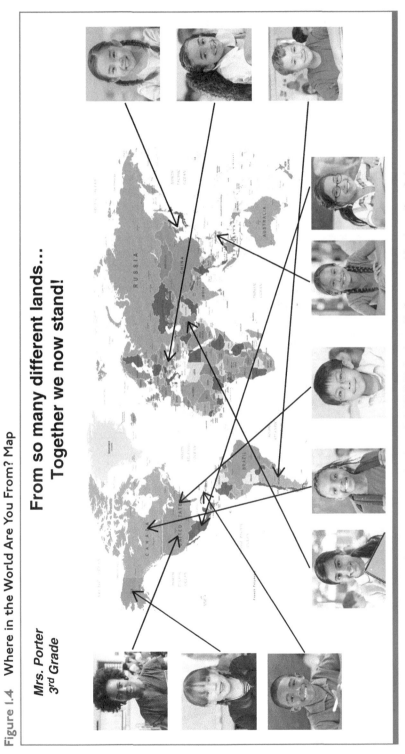

Figure 1.5   Country and Flag Graph

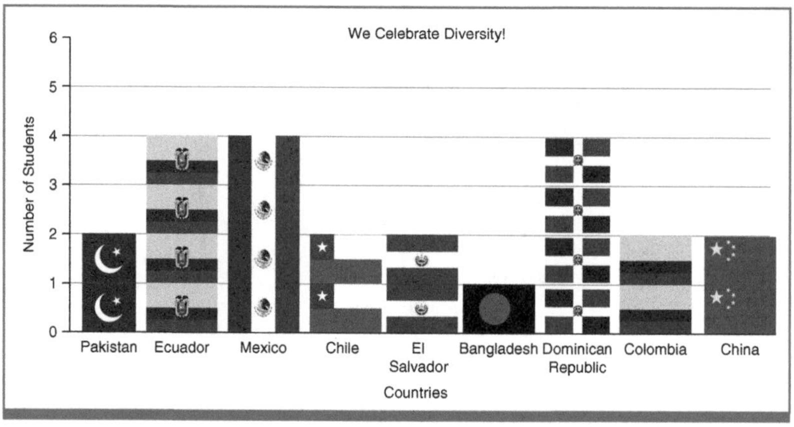

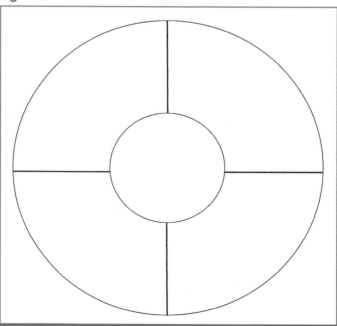

We Celebrate Diversity!

Sources: pixabay.com/kevin93sqs, pixabay.com/Clker-Free-Vector-Images, pixabay.com/
OpenClipart-Vectors, pixabay.com/tarcisiofbarbosa0, pixabay.com/mayns82

- <u>Standards based skills:</u> *oral language development, reading and interpreting graphs*

3. CULTURAL MANDALA

Put students in groups of three or four. Give them a mandala template as shown in Figure 1.6. Ask students to draw a picture of one or more objects or celebrations that represent their family and culture in one of

Figure 1.6   Cultural Mandala

the outer sections. Encourage them to use their first languages in their labels and descriptions. Then, in the inner section, have students draw the celebrations or objects they have in common. Each group shares their mandala, and mandalas remain on display around the room.

- Standards based skills: *oral language development, compare and contrast, appreciation and tolerance for cultural differences*

4. LANGUAGES WE SPEAK GRAPH.

In an activity much like the country and flag graph activity, ask students to raise their hands if they speak a language other than English. List the languages on the board. Graph the responses on a large sheet of paper and post it in the room under the title "Languages We Speak." Next to each of the languages, ask students to write greetings or words representing cultural celebrations in their home languages.

- Standards based skills: *oral language development, compare and contrast, appreciation and tolerance of cultural and linguistic differences*

5. LANGUAGES WE READ AND WRITE CORNER.

Ask students if they read and/or write another language. For students who do read and/or write another language, ask them to bring from home a book and/or a sample of something written in the language. Place these objects in a corner of the room and ask students to tell about what they brought. Leave these in the room for a period of time so that other students can look at them and talk together about them.

- Standards based skills: *oral language development, compare and contrast, appreciation and tolerance of cultural and linguistic differences*

Understanding Language Proficiency

Once you have determined where students in your classroom come from and whether they speak, read, and/or write a language other than English, you should also consider their language proficiency in English. While you may be aware of most newcomers, you might not be aware of how well those students and other emergent bilinguals in your class understand, read, write, or speak English. We suggest familiarizing yourself with the levels of English language proficiency (or English Language Development) used in your state/district/school (see Figures 1.7 and 1.8).

The table below lists adaptations of English language proficiency categories from the TESOL International Organization (formerly the Teachers of English to Speakers of Other Languages), California's English Language Development Standards, Engage New York's EL and Native Language Speakers language progressions, the Texas English Language Proficiency Levels, and the WIDA (World-class Instructional Design and Assessment) language proficiency level descriptors. Complete descriptions of the categories appear on the websites of each of these organizations.

Figure 1.7   English Language Proficiency Categories and Descriptions

TESOL	*Starting:* Limited or no understanding of English	*Emerging:* Understand and use phrases simple structures	*Developing:* Understand more complex language; need background to understand texts	*Expanding:* Understand basic communication; may read fluently but understand only basic facts in texts	*Bridging:* Show command of academic and social language
California ELD Standards		*Emerging:* Use English for immediate needs. Begin to understand and use academic language		*Expanding:* Increasing use of English in more contexts and learning more vocabulary and linguistic structures	*Bridging:* Moving to grade-level tasks and texts. Still need scaffolding
New York ESL Progressions	*Entering:* Does not meet linguistic demands of grade level	*Emerging:* Lacks proficiency to meet linguistic demands of grade level	*Transitioning:* Not yet meeting linguistic demands of grade level in academic contexts	*Expanding:* Approaching linguistic demands of grade level in academic contexts	*Commanding:* Has met the linguistic demands of grade level academic work

Texas English Language Proficiency Levels					
Beginning: Understands little or no English			*Intermediate:* Understands simple English in routine academic and social settings	*Advanced:* With support, understands and uses grade-level academic English	*Advanced High:* With minimal ESL support, understands and uses grade-level academic English

WIDA Language Proficiency Levels					
Entering: Pictorial or graphic representation of the language of the content areas; words, phrases, or chunks of language	*Beginning:* General language related to the content areas; phrases or short sentences	*Developing:* General and some specific language of the content areas; expanded sentences in oral interaction or written paragraphs	*Expanding:* Specific and some technical language of the content areas; a variety of linguistic complexity in oral and written language	*Bridging:* The technical language of the content areas; extended oral or written discourse, including stories, essays, or reports	*Reaching:* Specialized or technical language of the content area at grade level extended oral or written discourse as required by the specified grade level

COMPARE/CONTRAST MATRIX

Find out how the proficiency levels of students in your school are determined. Then, working in small groups, complete the compare/contrast chart below:

Figure 1.8   Compare/Contrast Matrix

Proficiency Level Descriptors	Are the categories the same as the ones used at your school? In what ways are they the same?	Are the categories different from the ones used at your school? In what ways are they different?
TESOL		
California		
New York		
Texas		
WIDA		

- Standards based skills: *compare and contrast, formulate opinions, analyze, evaluate*

- Classroom activities for a compare/contrast matrix:

  1. *This activity works well for comparing/contrasting two stories, characters, settings, historical events, or content concepts, such as climates, habitats, plants, animals, and so on.*

Assessing Students' English Language Proficiency

Teachers should be aware of their English learners' English language proficiency as they prepare lessons and teach. In order to plan, they should have some idea of the types of support students will need and what students can be expected to do at the different levels. Different states (and sometimes districts) offer specific ideas for how to support English learners at various proficiency levels. Schools may also assess English learners' proficiency in their home language using a scale similar to the ones above. If your school or district assesses students' home language proficiency, collect that assessment data for your English learners. This book provides scaffolding activities for English learners; however, keep in mind that, for beginning or emerging English learners, extra supports may also be necessary. In addition, it is important to be aware that some students may have suffered trauma through displacement, violence, and discrimination. These factors also may influence students' language development.

I-Search Project

Following the I-Search process of inquiry, search online to find out how your state or district determines language proficiency levels. Next, look at the suggestions provided for supporting English learners at those different levels. As you conduct this inquiry, answer the following I-Search questions:

1. What do I want to know about how to meet the needs of my ELs who are at different levels of English language proficiency?

2. What answers was I able to find in my search?

3. How can I record and use this information?

4. How can I share this information with others?

5. What did I learn about my students and about doing this kind of research?

6. What do I plan to do to differentiate instruction for ELs at different proficiency levels?

Like other strategies we suggest that you do, I-Search is an especially helpful strategy to use with students at more advanced levels of English proficiency.

- <u>Standards based skills</u>: *do research, use evidence to support ideas, create, summarize, explain*

- <u>Classroom activities for an I-Search:</u>
    I. *This activity can be used for any topic students are studying. Students could be given the first five questions and changing the first and fifth questions to reflect the research topic: What do I want to know about . . .? What did I learn about . . .?*

On Demand Writing Sample to Determine English Proficiency

Choose some English learners in your class you would like to know more about. Give them a general topic that students would have an opinion about. For example, you could ask them what they like to do outside school or what they like or don't like about school. Then ask all the students to write in English about the topic for a set amount of time, but at least for ten minutes. These samples should give you a general idea of the students' English literacy level. You can also ask students to write about a topic in their home language. Even if you can't read what they write, you can gauge their general ability in the language based simply on how much they write. Looking at their handwriting in either English or their home language will also give you an idea of how much formal schooling the student has received. Usually, students who have attended school have been given some formal instruction in penmanship.

Teachers can share their students' writing samples with other teachers to compare and contrast and analyze writing samples together. They can discuss writing samples, looking at students with same home languages and different home languages and considering students' length of residence in this country and previous schooling. Teachers can refer to the proficiency level descriptors to determine their students' written proficiency level.

- <u>Standards based skills:</u> *analyze, evaluate, use evidence to support ideas*

USING FORMATIVE ASSESSMENT

The On Demand writing sample is a good example of formative assessment. Formative assessments are designed to help teachers determine students' current ability in order to plan the next steps in instruction. MacDonald and her colleagues (2015) state that formative assessment "occurs in the midst of instruction and compares students' ongoing progress to possible trajectories of learning. It can help identify the most productive next steps in instruction" (p. xi). Formative assessment is one component of an overall assessment system that also includes interim and summative assessments.

MacDonald and her coauthors describe a four-stage process they use to integrate formative assessment into teaching. The first step is to design and teach lessons that have a consistent focus on developing both academic content knowledge and academic language. These lessons have clearly stated language objectives. The second step is to sample students' language by planning lessons during which students will produce language in oral or written form that can be collected. In the third step, teachers analyze student language samples. They use different tools to conduct their analyses and use this information to plan further instruction. The final step is to provide formative feedback. As MacDonald et al. comment, this stage is designed to

> give students clear, progress-oriented, and actionable information about their language use—both what they're doing well and what they can do to become more effective users of English—and to adjust instruction to meet students' needs. (p. xix)

The four steps form a cycle. The teacher plans instruction, gathers language samples, analyzes the samples, and provides formative feedback.

Teachers who use formative feedback develop different tools to assess language for formative purposes. Three useful tools are checklists, rating scales, and rubrics. Checklists contain items that students or teachers can respond to with a simple "yes" or "no." For example, with a checklist a student or a teacher could answer questions like "Did I use descriptive adjectives?" or "Did I write complete sentences that start with a capital letter?" Checklists are very useful when students self-assess.

A rating scale moves beyond "yes" and "no" to indicate how well something was done. For example, the teacher or a student could decide whether the writing contained many descriptive adjectives, some descriptive adjectives, or no descriptive adjectives. Similarly, the rating scale could ask if all the sentences were complete, most were complete, or some were complete.

Rubrics are more detailed than rating scales. They outline the criteria students should meet in different areas. Figure 1.9 shows a possible rubric for a short descriptive writing assignment.

Figure 1.9   **Writing Rubric**

Descriptive adjectives	Does not include effective descriptive adjectives	Uses some effective descriptive adjectives	Uses several effective descriptive adjectives
Complete sentences	Has several sentences that are not complete	Most of the sentences are complete	All of the sentences are complete
Capital letters and periods	A few of the sentences begin with a capital letter and end with a period	Most of the sentences begin with a capital letter and end with a period	Each sentence begins with a capital letter and ends with a period

Developing checklists, rating scales, and rubrics helps teachers make their expectations clear to their students, helping students know exactly what they need to do to succeed. These types of assessment can be used by teachers, by students working in pairs or small groups to assess one another's work, or by individual students.

In many schools, student-led conferences are a type of formative self-assessment used so that students can explain their current work to their parents or guardians. Figure 1.10 shows one young student discussing his work portfolio with his mother.

Figure 1.10   **Student-Parent Conference**

Develop a Formative Assessment

We have suggested several ways teachers can use assessment to inform instruction. Get together with others who are teaching the same materials as you are and develop a simple formative assessment you could use with your students. Some of these can be effectively used by the students themselves as a self-assessment, as explained above.

Using a Gradual Release of Responsibility Model

One way to support reading and writing development for English learners at different levels of language proficiency is to use a gradual release of responsibility model. In this way, students who are less proficient receive more support either from the teacher or a more capable peer as they acquire more proficiency in reading and writing English. In the model below, beginning ELs receive lots of support from their teacher or a more capable peer, and then, little by little, they move toward independence. This model is also recommended for use with students whose home language is English.

The gradual release of responsibility model of reading and writing (Pearson and Gallagher 1983) involves several steps. Effective instruction involves gradually releasing responsibility from the teacher to the student. At first, the teacher performs the task and the student observes and begins to engage with it. Next, the teacher helps the student perform the task. Gradually, the teacher removes the support and releases the responsibility so that the student can complete the task independently. Figure 1.11 shows how the gradual release model is applied to literacy instruction.

Instruction moves from teacher support (the area below the diagonal line) to student independence (the area above the line). As the figure shows, responsibility for reading and writing rests at first entirely with the teacher. The teacher models reading by reading books aloud or telling stories. Read alouds and storytelling model for students how

Figure I.II   Gradual Release of Responsibility Model

Teacher and Peer Support	⟶			Student Independence
Read Aloud	Shared Reading	Interactive Reading	Guided Reading	Independent Reading
Storytelling				
Modeled Writing	Shared Writing	Interactive Writing	Guided Writing	Independent Writing

texts are structured and introduce the academic vocabulary and syntax of written language. A teacher models writing by engaging students in language experience as students dictate stories or information. The students can see their oral language being written down, and then the students and the teacher read the writing together.

During the next stage, the teacher and students take joint responsibility for reading and writing. In shared reading, teachers often use big books so all the students can see the text. Teachers track the text as they read, and students chime in on predictable repeated sections. Interactive reading and writing may be done with the teacher or with peers. For example, teachers may read a text and have students echo what they read. The teacher may stop at certain sections so a student can continue the reading, and then the teacher may come back in. Interactive reading is often done in bilingual pairs, with one student assisting the other during the reading. During interactive writing, the teacher may sit with the student and help as needed as the student writes, or two students may work together on developing a piece of writing.

For guided reading and writing, the teacher may begin by presenting a mini-lesson to illustrate a particular skill or strategy. In guided reading, the teacher sits with small groups of students who all have a copy of the text. Students take turns reading to practice certain skills, such as predicting or using context to infer the meaning of unfamiliar words. In guided writing, the teacher works with a small group to help with specific writing skills, such as writing a good lead or deciding where to break a text into paragraphs. During guided reading and writing, the students take responsibility to read and write, focusing on certain skills under the teacher's guidance. The final step is for students to read and write independently. Teachers should allow time for independent reading and writing each day.

Wonderfilled Way of Learning

Choose a reading from your basal program and try out the gradual release model for that selection with a group of students. After you do this, answer the following questions based on the "Wonderfilled Way of Learning," developed by Don Howard (Freeman & Freeman, 1992).

1. What do I know about my students' reading abilities?

2. What do I wonder about which level of support I should offer to my English learners?

3. How can I find out about how they respond to the support?

4. Plan of Action: How will I proceed to apply the gradual release model effectively for my English learners?

   - <u>Standards based skills:</u> *draw on background knowledge, infer/ predict, create*

   - <u>Classroom activities for the "Wonderfilled Way of Learning":</u>

     1. *This activity can be used to have students explore any topic using the four question starters listed above.*

Drawing on Students' Backgrounds and Cultures

It is important to draw on what students already know about topics they will be studying. Marzano (2004) has conducted research showing that drawing on or building background is one of the most important practices teachers can use. If students already have knowledge on a topic that they developed in their home language, they may be able to access the knowledge more effectively if they are encouraged to draw on their home language resources.

Different introductory activities are excellent for helping to activate students' previous knowledge and to share with their peers knowledge they already have. Below we list a sampling of preview activities, activities students can use before reading that activate students' background knowledge.

1. GRAFFITI WALL

Have students write or draw anything they know about a topic on a large piece of butcher paper or a section of the classroom whiteboard. They can add relevant words in their home language. Read and discuss the entries together as a class.

- <u>Standards based skills:</u> *draw on background knowledge, create, ask probing questions*

2. GALLERY WALK

Put pictures related to the unit to be studied around the room. For example, if the unit is on life cycles, put up pictures or charts of the life cycles of different animals, insects, plants, and humans. Have students walk around the room and write comments on a sheet of paper under each of the pictures. Students can add what they know about the picture or write questions they have. They may also use their home languages to do this.

- <u>Standards based skills:</u> *draw on background knowledge, ask probing questions*

3. FOUR CORNERS

Put a different picture related to the unit readings in each corner of the classroom. If studying oceans, for example, pictures could show animals that live in the sea, a beach, a coral reef, and garbage floating in the ocean. Students go to the picture that most interests them. Next, each group talks about their pictures. After a certain amount of time, each group reports back to the class what they know about the subject of the picture and any questions they have about it.

- <u>Standards based skills:</u> *analyze, evaluate, formulate opinions, support ideas with evidence*

4. INQUIRY CHARTS

Ask students what they know about a topic and what they want to learn. Record students' ideas and put their names after their responses. Revisit the chart throughout the unit. Students can add things they have learned and additional questions they have.

- <u>Standards based skills:</u> *draw on background knowledge, explain*

Drawing on Students' Home Languages—Translanguaging

The common-sense practice that has been widely used in both ESL and bilingual classrooms is to keep students' home languages separate from instruction in English. During ESL classes, teachers and students only speak English. In many bilingual classes, only English is used in designated English time and Spanish or another language is used exclusively during the time designated for that language. Teachers have been encouraged not to mix languages as they teach. However, research supports the use of students' home languages to help them learn English and to learn academic content in English (Creese & Blackledge, 2010; Cummins, 2007; García, 2009). The practice of using both languages in instruction is referred to as translanguaging.

Research in sociolinguistics has shown that in bilingual communities, people regularly use both their home language and the language of the country. In many communities in the United States, it is common to hear people speaking English and Spanish, English and Korean, English and Arabic, or English and Mandarin. In addition, research in neurolinguistics has shown that, in bilingual people, both (or all) their languages are always active, a bit like an application that continues to run in the background on a smartphone.

Based on extensive observations in classrooms with English learners, García, Johnson, and Seltzer (2017) have shown that teachers can make strategic use of students' home languages as a scaffold to help them develop academic English proficiency. Based on this research, García and her colleagues have developed a theory of dynamic bilingualism. They explain:

> We use the metaphor of the translanguaging *corriente* to refer to the current or flow of students' dynamic bilingualism that runs through our classrooms and schools. Bilingual students make use of the translanguaging *corriente* either covertly or overtly to learn content and language in school and to make sense of their complex worlds and identities. (21)

Instead of looking at bilinguals as two monolinguals in one person, García (2009) argues that bilinguals have just one language repertoire, and the use of either language adds to this reservoir of language. Students can draw on this reservoir to make sense of instruction, read complex texts, and discuss and write about them.

Picture, then, a classroom of students. In it there are students of several different language backgrounds. As a class is conducted in English, a kind of invisible current of students' knowledge in their home languages is running, and bilingual children, when allowed and encouraged, can draw on their full linguistic repertoire to make sense of the instruction in English.

TRANSLANGUAGING STRATEGIES

Throughout this book, we will describe translanguaging strategies that both monolingual and bilingual teachers can use to scaffold instruction for emergent bilinguals in mainstream classes with English learners. Using translanguaging strategies not only scaffolds instruction but also affirms students' bilingual identities and their culture.

I. TURN AND TALK

In our first reflective activity, we asked you to turn and talk with a partner to discuss different topics. In classes with emergent bilinguals, teachers can ask students to do a turn and talk using either their home language or English. This allows all students to draw on all their language resources as they discuss lesson ideas. They can report back to the class in English.

Allowing students to choose the language during a turn and talk can be extended to any small-group discussion time. Teachers may want to put students who share the same home language together for pair or group work. At other times, teachers might create groups of students with different home languages. The benefit of using linguistically homogeneous groups is that students may be able to communicate more fully and expand their language ability. On the other hand, if the groups are linguistically mixed, then some of the students will be encouraged to communicate in the language they are just beginning to acquire.

- Standards based skills: *draw on background knowledge, explain, summarize*

2. COGNATE AND MULTILINGUAL WORD WALLS

A second translanguaging strategy is to draw on cognates and to make bilingual or multilingual word walls. This strategy helps build a multilingual linguistic ecology and also scaffolds instruction. Of course, there are no cognates if the home language is not related to English. However, about three-fourths of emergent bilinguals are Spanish speakers, and it is estimated that 30–40% of all English words have a related word in Spanish. Further, academic terms in English are often cognates of everyday Spanish words.

Teachers can draw on cognates in different ways. For example, students could be given a text in English and the translation in Spanish. Then, working in pairs, students could identify words that look alike. Next, students could report these words back to the teacher, who could make a chart of all the cognate pairs in the passage. Word walls with cognates based on terms from a unit of study can be posted around the room to serve as a resource for students as they talk, read, and write about the unit.

- <u>Standards based skills:</u> *compare and contrast, draw on background knowledge*

In classes with students who speak languages other than Spanish, the word walls can be expanded to include words from Mandarin, Arabic, or other languages. Multilingual word walls might include words that are not cognates but rather important terms related to the unit. All students are interested in seeing how their classmates write and pronounce words in their home language.

- <u>Standards based skills:</u> *draw on background knowledge, compare English and other languages*

3. USE BILINGUAL BOOKS

A third translanguaging strategy is to find and use bilingual books. Many bilingual books, both fiction and informational, are available in Spanish and English, for example. Emergent bilinguals can read a bilingual book in their home language to learn the content the class is studying. In addition, they can read the book in English and use the home language version of the text as a resource, much like a dictionary. They could also first read the text in their home language and then, with the background the text provides, try reading it in English.

Teachers who implement translanguaging strategies should use the two languages strategically. Simply translating everything does not help students develop proficiency in an additional language. Opportunities for including the two languages should be carefully planned. Students can draw on their home language to scaffold learning in English, but they also need time to speak, read, and write English to develop academic English proficiency.

CONCLUSION

Many mainstream teachers who have English learners in their classes are expected to teach using district-adopted language arts textbooks. These materials may include a few suggestions for working with English learners, but textbooks are written for native English speakers. Our goal in this book is to show how teachers can adopt a new approach and use strategies and key practices that make language arts units of inquiry based on big questions accessible to both native English speakers and English learners.

The key points for working effectively with emergent bilinguals that we have discussed include:

- Organizing your language arts curriculum around units of inquiry
- Getting to know your English learners so you can best teach them
- Creating a multilingual/multicultural environment
- Understanding the language proficiency of your students
- Using a gradual release of responsibility model of reading and writing
- Drawing on English learners' background knowledge
- Drawing on students' home languages (translanguaging)

The goal of this book is to give you the support you need to work effectively with the emergent bilingual students in your language arts classroom, using an approach that will make your language arts curriculum accessible to all of your students. Using this approach, you will see how to include both language and content objectives connected to Standards, how to make what you teach comprehensible to all your students, and how to choose appropriate texts for your students. When you use this approach, your English learners can develop the academic language and the academic content they need for school success.

Example Units

In Part Two, we describe four units of study. Two of the units are presented for lower elementary grades with additional ideas provided if the units are to be taught in higher grades. The other two units are geared toward upper elementary grade students but can be adapted to lower grades as well.

We introduce each chapter with key understandings for teachers as they plan their units. Chapter 2, a lower-grade unit on seeds, plants, and plant growth, includes a discussion of language objectives, what they are, and how to develop them. Chapter 3 is an upper-grade unit that centers on habitats. That chapter emphasizes the importance of providing comprehensible input for English learners in English language arts programs and includes a checklist of ways to make the input comprehensible. Chapter 4 is a lower-grade unit centered on the theme of oceans. In this chapter, we discuss the characteristics of texts that support readers, especially English learners. In our final chapter, we present an upper-grade unit on the Earth and the extreme weather that changes and endangers it. In this chapter, we explain academic language and emphasize the importance of teaching both academic language and academic content. We also come back to one of the main themes of the book, organizing curriculum around units of inquiry.

We describe the language arts units based on anchor texts from often-adopted language arts programs, and we provide strategies, as well as content and language objectives connected to the Standards. In addition, at the end of each chapter, there is a listing of the anchor books found in the basal programs. We also list a number of other books teachers working with students at different grade levels and different levels of English proficiency can draw upon as they teach the unit. Additionally, we list books in Spanish for teachers to use for previewing and reviewing lessons within the unit, using a translanguaging strategy.

We realize teachers may not have access to some resources we list, but our hope is that teachers will work with their librarian to order some of the texts we list. Librarians often ask teachers for book suggestions, and the lists in these chapters are a useful resource. Local public libraries may also have these books available, and some may be available as read alouds online.

After we describe in detail how one teacher developed each unit, we provide an outline of the strategies used within the lessons of the unit plus a brief description of each for quick reference. For those strategies that are only appropriate for lower elementary, we offer an alternative activity for upper-grade students. Similarly, for upper-grade units, we provide some strategy suggestions for lower-grade students. Printable online resources are included for many of the strategies.

CHAPTER TWO

Language Objectives
A Seeds, Plants, and Plant Growth Unit

In this chapter, we describe a lower-grade unit on seeds, plants, and plant growth to show how teachers can use the Equitable Access Approach for teaching emergent bilinguals in a mainstream class-room. Seeds, plants, plant growth, and products from plants are topics commonly covered in basal and alternative comprehensive literacy programs at different grade levels.

LANGUAGE OBJECTIVES

There is an increasing awareness that all teachers are teachers of both academic language and academic content. In fact, ESEA guidelines for English learners state that "it is crucial to the success of ELs that teachers are trained on how to support both ELs' English language development and their mastery of academic content knowledge" (U.S. Department of Education, 2016, p. 25). During lesson planning, teachers should write both content objectives and language objec-tives. Content objectives specify the academic content students are expected to learn, while language objectives are based on the language students will need as they read, write about, and discuss content. To write language objectives, teachers need to understand the differences between academic language and conversational language.

Academic language is a register of language that has developed to communicate concepts effectively in the different academic content areas. Cummins (2008) conducted research showing that English learners develop two types of language proficiency—academic language proficiency and basic communicative language skills.

As they communicate with native English speakers, watch movies and TV, or use social media, ELs acquire basic communicative skills. However, to succeed in school, all students, both ELs and native English speakers, need to acquire academic language. In mainstream classes that include emergent bilinguals it is important for teachers to plan and teach both academic language and academic content.

Cummins pointed out that basic communicative skills are context embedded and cognitively undemanding. For example, a student might talk with a classmate about how the weather in his new country is different from the weather at home. The concepts are not complex, and because the student has lived in these two places the context is embedded in her personal experience. On the other hand, academic language is less context embedded and more cognitively demanding. For example, as students write about plot development in a novel, they deal with an abstract concept rather than with their personal experiences, so the language is context reduced. In addition, students are expected to understand technical terms, such as *conflict, rising action,* and *resolution.* This makes writing about the plot more cognitively demanding. Academic language that is more context reduced and cognitively demanding than basic communication takes five to seven years for emergent bilinguals to develop.

Academic language includes specialized, technical vocabulary. This vocabulary includes words like *rectangle, evaporation, migration,* and *point of view.* In addition to content-specific vocabulary, academic language includes general vocabulary used across disciplines, words such as *analyze, conclude, define,* and *categorize.* As teachers teach the different content areas, they introduce students to academic language by teaching both content-specific and general academic language and the concepts they represent. Teachers can introduce these words and phrases as they teach the different content areas. They can also have students keep an academic vocabulary notebook. As they read and discuss their language arts texts, students should add to their notebooks the academic words and phrases that they find. Then they can refer to this notebook as they complete reading and writing assignments.

In addition to academic vocabulary, academic language has features that distinguish it from everyday language. It is more abstract, and more ideas are packed into each sentence. Academic texts are organized in certain ways. For example, in language arts, short stories, novels, plays, and poems each have their own organizational patterns and features. Texts in the different content areas are organized differently and have different components. A book report in language arts is different from a lab report in science. In order to learn language arts content, students need to develop the academic language of language arts.

To help students develop academic language proficiency, it is important for teachers to be aware that they are teaching both language and content in every lesson. To ensure this, teachers can write content objectives and language objectives. As they write content objectives, teachers can refer to the content-specific academic vocabulary that represents key concepts students should learn. For example, a content objective for language arts might be that students will identify the point of view the author uses in a short story the class is reading. To write language objectives, teachers begin with their content objective and then ask themselves, "What language forms and functions will students need as they read, write, and discuss this academic content?"

For example, in teaching a short story or a novel, a teacher might have as one content objective that students will be able to describe the main character in the story. A language objective based on this content objective could be that students will use descriptive adjectives to describe the character. A different language objective for students with higher levels of English proficiency could be that students will describe the main character using an adjective clause ("Mr. Smith, who was very tall, is the main character"). Teachers could use sentence frames to teach this objective ("Mr. Smith, who_____, is the main character"). Or the language objective might be to describe a character by writing a paragraph with a main idea (Mr. Smith was selfish) and supporting details (he wouldn't share his fortune with his children). As these examples and the examples that follow show, language objectives can be written at different levels.

At the beginning level, students can write simple sentences that start with a capital letter and end with a period. Students can write *wh*-questions *(Why did boy run away?)* that end with a question mark. Students can add adjectives or prepositional phrases to nouns *(an old man with a beard)*. They can add adverbs to verb phrases *(ran fast)*.

As emergent bilinguals become more proficient, they can write complex sentences. They can use signal words to show the relationships between clauses *(I ate dinner after I played with my friends)*. Students can write paragraphs in which each sentence connects with the main idea. They can also write texts that include the components of an academic genre (a haiku or a short story). In each case, the language objective is based on the content objective and represents some aspect of language used in reading, writing about, or discussing the academic content. As we describe the units of inquiry in each chapter, we include language objectives for some of the activities. While teaching traditional grammar has not been shown to be effective for improving students' English skills, teaching language directly related to academic content can help all students achieve higher levels of academic language proficiency. As we describe how Rosa teaches a unit on seeds, plants, and plant growth, we include examples of content and language objectives Rosa uses as she teaches the lessons.

PUTTING THE UNIT INTO CONTEXT: ROSA'S SEEDS, PLANTS, AND PLANT GROWTH UNIT

Rosa is a third-year elementary school teacher working in a large city in Texas. Some of her students began school in pre-kindergarten as non-English speakers. Although the majority of her ELs are native Spanish speakers, she also has students whose first languages include Arabic, Vietnamese, and Chinese. About half of her students are native English speakers. Rosa believes it is important to teach her multilingual students by organizing her curriculum around units of inquiry and teaching both academic language and academic content. She also draws on her students' primary languages and cultures. She knows that reading and writing taught with an emphasis on meaning-construction will help her ELs learn the academic English and the key concepts they need in the content areas.

Because she is required to teach language arts using the district-adopted basal reading program, she teaches the units the program includes and adapts her lessons to meet the needs of her students, both the native English speakers and the emergent bilinguals. She employs the key practices we outlined in our first chapter and writes both content objectives and language objectives for her lessons.

In Texas, the Standards come from the TEKS (Texas Essential Knowledge and Skills) that Rosa refers to as she plans. The science Standards for Rosa's grade level include carrying out field investigations, observing, recording, asking questions, and drawing conclusions. In addition, students should be able to observe nature and identify and label living things in nature. Students need to be able to identify parts of plants, what plants need, how plants grow, how we use plants, and plants in our environment.

Some of the language arts Standards can be met through carefully planned science content instruction. For example, the language arts Standards include using vocabulary that categorizes and describes sequences, dictating and composing informational text including procedural texts; reading both fiction and nonfiction; understanding the difference between fact and fiction; reading and making inferences using features of texts, such as charts and graphs; gathering and synthesizing information; creating mental images from information; participating in the reading of predictable books and poetry; and responding to readings through talk, art, and writing.

To meet these Standards, Rosa and the other teachers at her grade level plan a unit on plant growth answering the big question, "How does what we grow help us grow?" Sub-questions teachers want students to explore include, "What do plants need to live and grow?" "What are the stages of plant growth?" and "How long do seeds take to grow into plants?" The teachers share activity ideas and develop a unit that helps their students build academic literacy and content knowledge. During the unit, Rosa and her colleagues draw on books available in Spanish to use with Spanish-speaking ELs to preview and review the content of the texts they read in English.

PREVIEW ACTIVITIES: DRAWING ON AND BUILDING BACKGROUND

Identification of Seeds

Rosa starts her unit by bringing in a large jar that contains many different kinds of seeds (see Figure 2.1). She shows the jar to the class, walking around the room so that everyone can see what is in the jar. Then she asks, "What is in this jar?" Her students answer enthusiastically, "Seeds!" Then Rosa asks them if they can identify any of the seeds. Some children recognize corn, others recognize beans, pumpkin, and watermelon seeds. Some of her emergent bilinguals know the names of the seeds in their native language. As the English words are used, they begin to pick up the new vocabulary. A few children even recognize lettuce seeds and pepper seeds, explaining that they help their mothers plant those seeds in their family garden. As the children offer answers, Rosa fills in a circle graph (see Figure 2.2), writing the word *seeds* in the middle and then filling in the names of the seeds the children identify in the circles that radiate out from the center.

Figure 2.1   Picture of Seeds

Source: Pixabay.com/PublicDomainPictures

Figure 2.2   Circle Graph

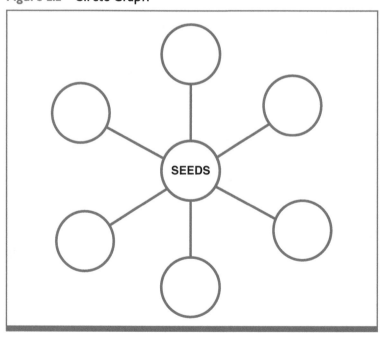

After the circle graph is completed, Rosa asks her students to write a sentence. She puts a sentence frame on the board: "Three kinds of seeds are _____, _____, and _____." She points out that writers use commas to separate words in a list. Then she gives students time to write their sentences.

- <u>Standards based skills:</u> *completing graphs, creating mental images from information, observing, identifying and labeling*
- <u>Content objective:</u> *Students will be able to identify different types of seeds.*
- <u>Language objective:</u> *Students will separate words in a list with commas as they write the names of the seeds they identify.*

Classification of Seeds

Rosa puts her students into groups to help them further investigate seeds and types of seeds (see Figure 2.3). She organizes some groups with all native Spanish speakers and other groups with two or three members who speak other home languages. She encourages the children to speak their home languages if that helps them.

She gives each group a plastic baggie with a variety of seeds they have already seen in their first circle graph activity. She asks the children to glue all the same types of seed inside circles drawn on a sheet of paper and then label each circle with the name of the type of seed.

Next, Rosa gives each group a seeds classification chart (see Figure 2.4). Together, they chart a few types of seeds by listing color, shape, feel, and smell, if any. Before starting, they talk about some descriptive words for texture, like *bumpy, prickly, smooth, hard,* and *soft.* They also

Figure 2.3   Students Labeling Seeds

Figure 2.4 Classification of Seeds Chart

Kind of seed	Color of seed	Shape of seed	Texture How does it feel?	Does it have an odor? Does it smell?

talk about the odor or the smell. Students predict the seeds won't have much odor. The students then work together to fill in the rest of chart. Rosa has her groups share the answers on their charts and leads a class discussion on the characteristics of the different seeds.

Then Rosa asks the students to use the chart to write a sentence that shows the difference between two types of seeds. She writes a sentence frame on the board: "_____ seeds are _____ and _____, but _____ seeds are _____ and _____." She shows the class how to complete the sentence using a pumpkin seed and a lettuce seed as her example. She explains that they can use words like *but* to show how two things are different. She points out that words like *but* that connect two sentences are preceded by a comma.

- <u>Standards based skills:</u> *using descriptive words to categorize, completing a chart*
- <u>Content objective:</u> *Students will observe, draw conclusions, and record information.*
- <u>Language objective:</u> *Students will use coordinate conjunctions preceded by a comma to write compound sentence.*

Gallery Picture Walk

After building background for her students with the seed activities, Rosa collects pictures of different types of plants that grow from the seeds that the students identified earlier. She finds pictures in the library, in magazines, and on the Internet.

She posts the pictures around the classroom with a sheet of paper under each picture for students to write on. On a table, she puts the seeds into five piles and numbers each pile. Working together, pairs of students match the picture of each plant with the number of one of the piles of seeds; they write a sentence under the picture that identifies each plant and explains why they made their choice of the seed. Rosa asks them to use sentences with the word *because*. She gives them the example, "I chose seed number 3 for the sunflower picture *because* it is oval and has a white stripe."

After students have moved around the room writing what plants they see and the number of the seed for each plant, Rosa asks students to walk around the room again and read the answers their peers have written. This leads to a lively discussion about the plants and their seeds.

- Standards based skills: *draw on background knowledge, identifying and labeling*
- Content objective: *Students will identify plants and match the plants with their seeds.*
- Language objective: *Students will use complex sentences with* **because** *to explain cause and effect.*

AS WE ENGAGE IN THE UNIT: VIEW ACTIVITIES

KWL Chart

Rosa's students have done several preview activities that helped them build background knowledge as well as draw on information they already knew. For this reason, Rosa begins a KWL chart to leave up in the room while the class studies plants and seeds (see Figure 2.5). KWL charts organize what is **k**nown, what learners **w**ant to know, and what they've **l**earned. Rosa asks students to tell her, "What do we know about plants and seeds?" and "What do we want to learn about plants and seeds?" Rosa records the students' comments using their words and writes students' names next to their comments. Writing down the students' ideas in front of them helps all her students, especially her emergent bilinguals, develop language, and it helps them understand the content they are studying. As the unit progresses, the class returns to the chart using different-colored markers each time they write new information. Students also are asked to give the source of the new information they add. During the unit, they come back to the chart to fill in the "What we have we learned" section.

Figure 2.5 KWL Chart

What do we know about plants and seeds?	What do we want to learn about plants and seeds?	What have we learned about plants and seeds?

- <u>Standards based skills:</u> *draw on background knowledge, explain*
- <u>Content objective:</u> *Students will describe what they know about plants and seeds and generate questions for inquiry about plants and seeds.*
- <u>Language objective:</u> *Students will use complete sentences with a subject and a predicate. ("Plants grow from seeds.")*

Plant Growth Project

Rosa then explains to her students that they are going to grow their own seeds and observe their plants like scientists. Rosa tells the students they will choose two or three different seeds from the seeds they sorted at the beginning of their unit and grow their own plants. The students will observe their plants as they grow to discover under what conditions plants grow best. She explains they will keep a plant journal as their seeds grow.

Plant Growth Journal

The next day, the students choose the seeds they want to grow. Rosa encourages all the students to try beans because she knows they grow easily, but she also allows students to try any other seeds they are interested in growing. Students choose seeds like peas, corn, melon, and even tiny lettuce or carrot seeds. They dampen paper towels and add a small amount of bleach. The bleach keeps the seeds from becoming moldy. Next, they wrap individual seeds in the towels. Then they put each towel in a plastic bag. Rosa has students put one of their plastic bags on a windowsill where it will get sun and another of their plastic bags inside their desk where it is dark. Other students place one of their plastic bags in the classroom refrigerator.

Rosa passes out construction paper for students to make a plant journal cover and gives them pages to put in their journals, where they will record the growth of their plants (Figure 2.8 shows a sample journal page). The pages have space to draw the plant and then write one or two sentences. Over the next couple of weeks, students record in their plant journals where the seed had been located, as well as the date and the number of days since the seed was put into the wet paper towel. As part of the record showing how the seeds are sprouting, they also draw pictures of the plants and record their findings each time they observe each of their seeds. The students write what they notice about their sprouting seeds. Rosa works with the class to write examples of sentences students should use in their journals, such as *On the third day, I saw a white root with little hairs. On the fifth day, there was a stem and leaves.* As the students observe and record, Rosa takes pictures with an iPad of these early stages of plant growth that the students are observing and puts them on the bulletin board. She labels these pictures as shown in Figures 2.6 and 2.7.

Figure 2.7   **Students Draw and Record Seed Growth**

Figure 2.6   **Seeds Sprouting**

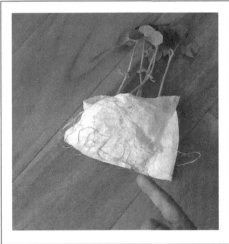

Figure 2.8   Template Pages for Student Journals

Date _____ How many days? _____ **Was your seed in the sun, dark, or cold?** _____ _____ **Describe how the seed has changed.** _____ _____ _____ _____ _____	**Draw the seed. Show how the seed changes.**

- Standards based skills: *conduct a simple descriptive investigation, collect data and make observations, demonstrate an understanding of information gathered*
- Content objective: *Students will record and organize data using pictures, words, and ordinal numbers.*
- Language objective: *Students will write complete sentences using past tense verbs, descriptive words, and ordinal numbers identifying seed growth. ("On the third day I saw a white root and little hairs.")*

During the unit, Rosa scaffolds student writing by using sentence frames and example sentences. She decides to conduct a formative assessment to see how well her students can write the sentences in their plant journals. She develops a rating scale to assess the students' use of the kind of sentences she would like them to write in their plant journal entries. The student entries should have complete sentences with past-tense verbs, descriptive words, and ordinal numbers. Figure 2.9 shows Rosa's rating scale.

Figure 2.9   Rating Scale for Plant Journal

Name: _____

Did the student...?	Not at all	Some of the time	Most of the time	All of the time
Write complete sentences				
Use past tense verbs				
Use descriptive words				
Use ordinal numbers				

Since Rosa wants the students to use the scale to evaluate their journal entries, she projects the scale so all the students can see it. After going over the items to be rated, she works through two examples of journal entries with the class. She asks them to decide how to evaluate each entry on the different criteria. When students show an understanding of how they are to mark the ratings, she has them form bilingual pairs and instructs them to each choose three entries from their plant growth journal to evaluate. The students work together to decide how to rate the entries. When all the pairs have finished, Rosa collects the rating sheets so she can also check them. This formative assessment helps Rosa identify her students' levels of English proficiency and also helps her plan upcoming lessons in her unit on plants and seeds.

Picture Walk With Anchor book: *Where Does Food Come From?*

The students work on their plant journals and also continue reading and talking about plants. Rosa shows the students one of the anchor books from her basal program, *Where Does Food Come From?* (Rotner & Goss, 2006). Together Rosa and the students do a picture walk through the book. As they turn the pages, they identify what they see on each page and make comments about the different types of food pictured in the text, including food from plants, like corn and tomatoes, and food that doesn't come from plants, like eggs, honey, syrup, and milk. Students comment on the foods they usually eat for breakfast, lunch, and dinner.

Next, Rosa reads the text to the students as they follow along in their anthologies. She then asks students to read the story to one another in pairs. She pairs her emergent bilinguals with native English speakers or another more English-proficient emergent bilingual. As they read, Rosa moves around the room listening to the students as they are reading the book and helping students who have questions. She then has the children respond to a Where Do Foods Come From? chart she gives to each pair (see Figure 2.10). First, Rosa asks the students to list the foods in the story and then decide where the foods come from. She tells students they may talk in their first language but should write their answers in English.

Figure 2.10   Where Do Foods Come From? Chart

Food	Plant? Animal? Insect?	Name of plant, animal, or insect	Where do you find it? Farm? Forest? Garden?

Rosa and the students then discuss the answers each group put on their charts to create a class chart.

After the class chart is complete, Rosa hands each group another book about plants and animals and what foods we get from them, including books like *Where Does Breakfast Come From?* (Flint, 1998), *Where Does Our Food Come From?* (Kaiman, 2011), *How Did That Get in My Lunchbox? The Story of Food* (Butterworth, 2013), and *Corn Crazy* (Woolley, 2012). She asks students in each group to read their book together and then fill out the Where Do Foods Come From? chart for the foods in their book. As students read their books and begin to fill out their charts, Rosa moves about the room helping students who need assistance.

Once the groups have completed their charts, students present their books and charts. First, students in each group take turns reading two pages of their book to the class. Then, they present their charts. After each presentation, other students make comments or ask questions.

- Standards based skills: *draw on background knowledge, synthesize information to create new information, demonstrate an understanding of new information*
- Content objective: *Students will demonstrate an understanding of information they have gathered about seeds and plants.*
- Language objective: *Students will describe information from a chart orally.*

Translanguaging Venn Diagram

Rosa asks her students if they remember a book they may have read in kindergarten, *The Carrot Seed* (Krauss, 2004). When she takes out the big book version, many of the students say they remember it. She reads the book with the students in a shared reading. The students chime in on parts of the text that are repeated. After reading *The Carrot Seed,* Rosa takes out another big book, *Una semilla nada más (Just One Seed)* (Ada, 1990). She tells students that this book in Spanish is very similar to *The Carrot Seed*. She explains to students who do not speak or understand Spanish that she is going to read the book in Spanish, and she wants them to remember the story of *The Carrot Seed*, look at the pictures, and decide what the story is about.

After reading the story, Rosa asks her English speakers if they understood what was happening. Most students say they did, and together they give her the summary of the story of a boy who planted a seed and took care of it. His mother, father, and sister didn't think it would grow. However, the boy continued to take care of the seed, and it grew until it became a huge sunflower.

Then, she asks all the students if they can tell her how the story is the same as or and different from *The Carrot Seed*. She leads the class to fill in a Venn diagram to compare and contrast the two books (see Figure 2.11). To build academic language through discussion, Rosa writes two sentence frames for students to use: "*A Carrot Seed* is the same as *Una semilla nada más* because ___" and "*A Carrot Seed* is different from *Una semilla nada más* because ___". She encourages the students to use these sentence frames as they point out similarities and differences.

The students note, for example, that both stories have a boy who planted a seed. Both stories have a mom and dad who don't believe the seed will grow. The boy in both stories takes care of the plant and waters it. However, in *The Carrot Seed*, the plant was a large carrot that grew under the ground and in *Una semilla nada más*, a huge sunflower grew above the ground. The students find other differences, including the fact that in *Una semilla nada más*, there is a sister in addition to a brother, and the story shows all the ways people use a sunflower. Although the books are written in two languages, the discussion and the class chart are completed in English. This translanguaging strategy helps students develop the ability to find differences and similarities, an important skill. In fact, Marzano, Pickering, & Pollock (2001) conducted research showing that finding similarities and differences is one of the most effective instructional strategies teachers can use to improve student learning.

Figure 2.11   Translanguaging Venn Diagram

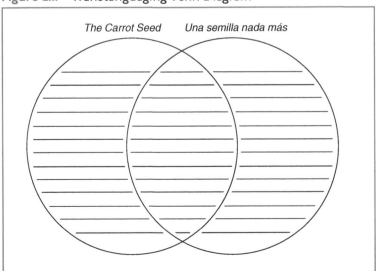

- <u>Standards based skills:</u> *compare and contrast facts from two stories*
- <u>Content objective:</u> *Students will compare and contrast details from two stories.*
- <u>Language objective:</u> *Students will use complex sentences with "same as" and "different from" to describe similarities and differences.*

Turn and Talk and Review KWL Chart

After the class finishes the Venn diagram, Rosa asks the students to look back at their KWL chart and tell her what they have learned so far about plants and seeds that was not already on the KWL chart and what new questions they have about plants and seeds. Students turn to a partner, and together the pair makes a list of what they have been learning that is not already on the chart. They talk about different foods we eat that come from plants, they talk about how plants that give food come from different places, and they talk about taking care of plants, including what the boys in *Una semilla nada más* and *The Carrot Seed* did to make the plants grow. They share what they have learned so far about the seeds they planted in their pocket gardens and the environments in which their seeds grew best. Partners also brainstorm new questions about plants and seeds. Rosa leads the class as they add more information to the KWL chart.

- <u>Standards based skills:</u> *draw on background knowledge, explain*
- <u>Content objective:</u> *Students will demonstrate an understanding of information they have gathered about seeds and plants and generate questions for inquiry about plants and seeds.*
- <u>Language objective:</u> *Students will be able to formulate* wh- *questions* (why, when, where, how, what).

Parts of Plants We Eat

The next day, Rosa brings some vegetables. She reminds students about their discussions of the plants we eat and the book *Where Does Food Come From*. She shows them a tray with a cauliflower, a bunch of broccoli, an artichoke, some carrots, a bunch of beets, a bunch of radishes, a stalk of celery, some stalks of asparagus, a cucumber, some cherry tomatoes, a head of cabbage, a head of lettuce, and a bunch of spinach. First, she asks the students if they know the names of these vegetables. Some of the English learners know the names in their home language but not in English, but working together as a class, the students identify all the vegetables. Rosa writes the names of the vegetables on the whiteboard. During the discussion, students comment on how much they like or dislike the various vegetables and how their parents prepare the vegetables.

Next, Rosa draws a huge flowering bean plant on a large piece of butcher paper. She labels the major parts, including flower, leaf, stem, seeds, and roots. Figure 2.12 shows an example of a flower with the main parts labeled.

Figure 2.12   Labeled Plant

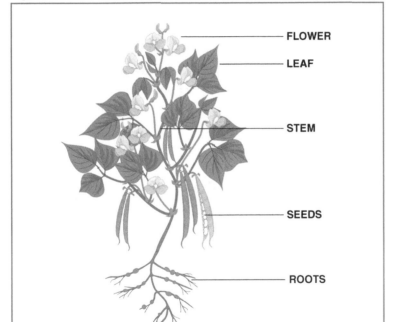

Source: iStock.com/mariaflaya

Next, she asks the students to help her decide what part of each vegetable on the tray that we eat. The class decides that we eat the leaves of lettuce, the stems of celery, and the roots of carrots. Rosa places those plants on that part of the bean plant she drew on the butcher paper. For example, she placed carrots next to "roots" on her drawing of the bean plant. During the activity, one student points out we eat the roots of beets but also the leaves, and another points out his mother uses celery leaves in soups. Students are interested that broccoli, artichokes, and cauliflower are really flowers we eat. The Mandarin speakers in her class point out that in their homes they eat a vegetable like broccoli but skinnier, and they explain that people eat the leaves too. Rosa finds pictures of broccolini on the Internet to show the whole class.

Following the discussion, Rosa asks her students to write two sentences, one telling three vegetables they like, and the other telling three they dislike. She reminds them that they should separate words in their lists with commas. When the pairs finish, they report their likes and dislikes to the class. Rosa posts the results up on the board. Then she leads a class discussion about which vegetables students in her class like most and which vegetables they dislike most.

Rosa has worked with the students to use commas to separate words in a list, so she uses a rating scale to quickly evaluate her students' completed sentences. This helps her decide how well students are progressing on this skill. Figure 2.13 shows Rosa's rating scale.

Figure 2.13   Rating Scale for Commas in List

Name	Did not use commas correctly	Used commas correctly some of the time	Used commas correctly most of the time	Used commas correctly all of the time

- Standards based skills: *draw on background knowledge, explain, categorize, make inferences*
- Content objective: *Students will demonstrate their understanding of parts of a plant connecting it to foods in their environment.*
- Language objective: *Students will write sentences about plants they like to eat and those they dislike with lists separated by commas.*

Predicting Vocabulary With Anchor Book *From Seed to Pumpkin*

Before reading the second anchor book in the basal reader, *From Seed to Pumpkin* (Pfeffer, 2015), Rosa asks her students to look at the book cover and read the title. Then, she asks the students to think about the activities that they have done with seeds and about the books they have already read about seeds and plants. Next, she asks the students to predict some words they think they will find when they read the story. Students first turn to a partner and talk together about some words, and then the whole class shares. Students suggest words and phrases like *ground, soil, plant a seed, sun, grow, water, leaves, flowers,* and *fruit.* Rosa writes those words on the board and then reads the story to the class as they follow along. Students raise their hands each time they notice a word they predicted.

- Standards based skills: *draw on background knowledge, predict in reading*
- Content objective: *Students will show an understanding of the stages of plant growth by naming key words that describe how a plant grows.*
- Language objective: *Students will build academic vocabulary related to plant growth listing key vocabulary.*

Sequence Stages of Growth Chart *From Seed to Pumpkin*

Rosa next gives the students a sequence chart (see Figure 2.14). Students work in pairs to draw and label the stages of growth of the pumpkin. The students look at the story and fill in the boxes on the chart by drawing and labeling in order of growth: seed, seedling, leaves, vine, bud, flower, small green pumpkin, and large orange pumpkin. Together they orally describe the steps using signal words from the story and some that they already know such as *first, next, then, after, in a few weeks, finally,* to describe the growth sequence. Rosa makes a list of the different signal words the class uses and puts them up on a large chart on the wall.

The next day, Rosa and her students review their sequence charts and together write a paragraph describing the growth of pumpkins using the information on their charts. They include the signal words on the wall chart that Rosa made to indicate the sequence and then read their paragraph together.

Figure 2.14   Sequence Chart

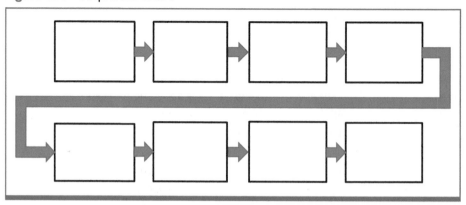

- <u>Standards based skills:</u> *identify information from a text, synthesizing information from a text*
- <u>Content objective:</u> *Students will demonstrate an understanding of the stages of the growth of a pumpkin from seed to pumpkin by locating the stages on a growth chart from a reading.*
- <u>Language objective:</u> *Students will use signal words orally and in writing to indicate sequence and make the paragraph more cohesive.*

Celery Stalk Root Absorption Activity

Rosa rereads the first pages of *From Seed to Pumpkin* that explain how the seed breaks up and how roots form tubes under the ground. These roots absorb water like straws. She also reads the part of the story where the author describes the pumpkin plant stems and how water moves in them. Rosa asks her students if they remember which of the vegetables she brought in were stems. They remember that the asparagus and celery were stems.

Rosa then explains they are going to do an experiment with celery to see how plants absorb liquid in the same way that we drink with a straw. She brings in three jars, a food-coloring kit, and some celery stalks with leaves. Rosa has the students help her put drops of red food coloring in one jar and blue and green food coloring in the other two jars. Then she chooses three students to put celery stalks in each jar (see Figure 2.15). Rosa explains the class will check each day to see if the stalks absorb the colored water. She gives them a sheet where they record, draw, and color what they observe each day (see Figure 2.16).

Over the next few days, the students check the celery stalks and record what they observe. They notice the leaves in the green water turned very green, and the leaves in the blue water turned blue. Only the tips of the leaves in the red water turned a bit red. The class determines that the red water solution must have been weak. To help her students fill in the part of the chart where they record their observations, Rosa explains that the students should write one complete sentence that starts with a capital letter and ends with a period to describe the celery in each jar.

Figure 2.15   Celery-Stalk Experiment

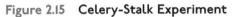

Figure 2.16   Celery Experiment Record Sheet

Day 1	Draw and color.	What did you observe?
Day 2	Draw and color.	What did you observe?
Day 3	Draw and color.	What did you observe?
Day 4	Draw and color.	What did you observe?

- Standards based skills: *carry out a field investigation, draw conclusions, observe, and record*
- Content objective: *Students will demonstrate an understanding of how plants absorb nutrients by observing and recording the results of a celery-stalk experiment.*
- Language objective: *Students will write complete sentences that start with a capital letter and end with a period. They will use the past tense, "I saw . . ." or "I observed . . .".*

REVIEW ACTIVITIES FOR PLANTS AND SEEDS UNIT

KWL Chart Review

To review key concepts the students have already learned about seeds and plant growth, Rosa has her students go to the section of the classroom library with different books on seeds and plants. In pairs, students choose books. Rosa encourages some of her less proficient English learners to read books like *Plants and Seeds; Plantas y semillas* (Walker, 1992a, 1995b), *Seeds Grow; Las plantas crecen* (Walker, 1992b, 1995a) and *Plants Grow From Seeds; De las semillas nacen las plantas* (Lucca, 2001, 2003). These limited-text books are accessible to all her students, including her ELs. They also have a Spanish version that Spanish-speaking students can refer to as they read the English version. She then asks student pairs to pick out a book together, read it, and go to the KWL chart. If their book contains information they already know and is already on the chart, they simply put a checkmark by that fact. If they learned something new, they write that information on the class chart. The pair also adds to the "What do you want to learn?" section if they have questions. In some cases, students draw on the information gained from reading in their home language and then complete the chart in English.

When the students have finished recording information and questions on the chart, Rosa shows them the Spanish and English versions of *Plants and Seeds*. She asks the students to work with their partner to find words in the Spanish version of the book that look like the same word in the English version. Students identify several words, such as *plants* and *plantas*. Rosa explains that many words in English and Spanish look alike, and that these words are called cognates. Then she works with the students to create a class cognate wall. She leaves the list up on the board and tells students they can add new words to the list when they read.

- Standards based skills: *gather and synthesize information from a text, respond in writing*
- Content objective: *Students will demonstrate an understanding of information they have read by recording that information on a KWL chart.*
- Language objective: *Students will add key vocabulary to the KWL chart. Emergent bilinguals will draw on cognates to build reading comprehension.*

How Long Do Seeds Take to Grow Into Plants?

Rosa moves from the KWL chart to the topic of how long seeds take to grow. As their own plants sprout and grow, the students now transfer those seeds into small clear plastic cups with soil. Rosa's students observe the transplanted healthy sprouts growing in soil over the coming two months. She reminds students about the books they have already read, including their anchor text *From Seed to Pumpkin* and *The Carrot Seed*. She asks them if the plants in those books took a short or long time to grow. They all agree that the pumpkins and carrots took a long time. She then reads *Growing Radishes and Carrots* (Bolton & Snowball, 1985), a content pop-up book that contrasts how long it takes radishes and carrots to grow. The students can clearly see that it took the carrots a lot longer to grow than the radishes.

To reinforce the stages of plant growth and how plants differ as they grow, Rosa then reads *I'm a Seed* (Marzollo, 1996), a story told from the point of view of two different seeds growing, one a flower and the other a pumpkin. The students discuss the steps of plant growth for each plant, and they also discuss the differences between fact and fiction. The part of the story telling about how the plants grow contains facts, but the students recognize that since the seeds talk to each other, there is also fiction in the story. Drawing on the information in all the books, Rosa and the students list the steps of plant growth.

- Standards based skills: *draw on background knowledge, distinguish between fact and fiction*
- Content objective: *Students will demonstrate an understanding of how long it takes different seeds to become plants and identify the stages of plant growth.*

- Language objective: *Students will identify what parts of the story* I'm a Seed *are fact and which are fiction. (In* I'm a Seed, *the plants talk. That is fiction. In* I'm a Seed, *the seeds sprout. That's fact.)*

MEASURING PLANT GROWTH

At the same time they are doing the various reading activities, Rosa's students continue to observe their plants and measure and graph their growth in different environments using the graphs she gives them for their plant journals (see Figures 2.17 and 2.18). The students compare the growth of their plants in different environments: sun, dark, and cold. At the end of the month, Rosa leads a class discussion. She asks, "Which plants grew best?" The students conclude that the seeds in the sun grew best, and the seeds kept in dark or cold places did not grow well at all. The students form comparative sentences like, *My bean seeds grew best in the sun. They grew taller than the seeds in the cold, and the roots were longer.*

Figure 2.17 Stem and Root Graph

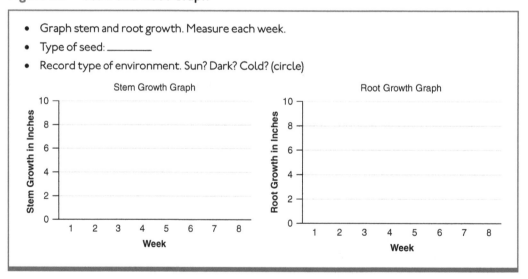

- Standards based skills: *communicate observations and provide reasons for explanations using student-generated data from simple descriptive investigations*
- Content objective: *Students will compare the growth of plants in different environments.*
- Language objective: *Students will use comparative adjectives to talk about how their plants grew. ("The corn seed grew taller in the sun. The bean seed had the tallest stem. The carrot seed had the longest root.")*

Figure 2.18   Measuring Plant Growth

Source: iStock.com/Sidekick

Writing a Procedure

Rosa wants to review with the students the steps they took during their plant growth experiment. She explains that scientists write down the steps to explain the procedure they followed so that other scientists can follow the same procedure. She leads the class in a discussion of the steps they took and writes them on a large piece of butcher paper as a paragraph:

"We chose three kinds of seeds. We moistened a paper towel with water mixed with a little bleach. We placed the seeds in the towel. We put the seeds and the towel in a plastic bag. We placed some of the seeds in the sun, some in a dark place, and some in a cold place. We observed the seeds three times a week. We recorded and drew the changes we saw in the seeds in our seed journal. We then planted the seedlings in soil. We measured the growth of the stems and roots each week. We drew conclusions based on our observations."

When they have finished recalling the steps of the experiment, Rosa asks them, "How would you tell someone how to do the experiment just the way you did it?" "How could you change what we have written here to a set of directions for finding out about the conditions under which plants grow best?" She leads a discussion to help the students change each sentence in the paragraph into a form they would use to tell someone what to do. She suggests they could write this as a list. With help from Rosa and using the information from the paragraph they brainstormed, the students develop the following list:

1. Choose three kinds of seeds.
2. Moisten a paper towel with water mixed with a little bleach.
3. Place the seeds in the towel.
4. Place the seeds and the towel in a plastic bag.
5. Place the plastic bag in the sun (or in a dark place, or in a cold place).
6. Observe the seed three times a week.
7. Record and draw the changes you see in the seeds in your seed journal.
8. Plant the seedlings in soil in a clear plastic cup.
9. Measure the growth of the stems and the roots.
10. Draw conclusions based on your observations.

When they finish the list, Rosa explains that this is similar to the way scientists report on procedures they have followed during an experiment. She asks the students to talk together about how the paragraph and the list are different from one another. Then she surveys the groups. They notice the difference between a paragraph and a numbered list. They also notice that the list items all start with a verb. They also point out that the paragraph used "we," but the list doesn't. Rosa concludes the discussion by telling the students that the list is called a scientific procedure and that they will be writing up more experiments later this year using this kind of procedure writing.

During their project with pocket gardens and growing sprouts in soil, Rosa took pictures of the various stages of plant growth with her iPad. Then to review the experiment with her students, Rosa has them work in groups to write answers to the questions: "What are the parts of a plant?" "What does a plant need to grow?" "What are the stages of plant growth?" and "How long do seeds take to grow into plants?" When they discuss plant growth, Rosa projects the pictures she has taken of the stages of their plants growing on the classroom Smart Board from her iPad. Students also refer to their graphs and charts in their own plant journals as Rosa shows the pictures.

- <u>Standards based skills:</u> *use vocabulary to explain sequence of events, compose procedure text, synthesize information*

- <u>Content objective:</u> *Students will carry out a field observation, observe and record data, label nature, identify what plants need to grow, label the stages of plant growth, and record how long plants take to grow.*
- <u>Language objective:</u> *Students will understand the components of the scientific procedure genre and write a procedure.*

All About Plants Book

To complete the unit and to ensure that the students draw on all they have learned through reading books, completing charts and graphs, and keeping their journals, Rosa tells the students they will work in pairs to make their own plant books. The books will include the pictures she has taken in the classroom of their seeds growing into plants and pictures the students will take. The students will write about the pictures for their books. In addition, the students will take pictures to complete their books.

Working in pairs, students go around the schoolyard and take pictures of plants and parts of plants using iPads the school provides for students. Rosa gives them page templates to fill in with pictures and words to describe the parts of plants and what plants need (see Figures 2.20 and 2.21). She also takes pictures of each pair for the cover of each book (see Figure 2.19).

Figure 2.19   *All About Plants* Book Cover

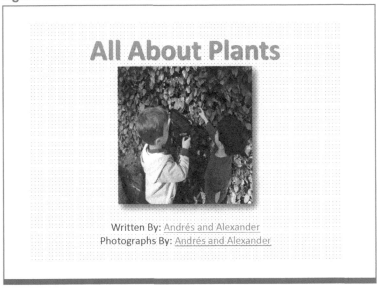

Figure 2.20   Book Page for Parts of Plants

These are the

_____

Figure 2.21   Book Page for What Plants Need

Plants need _____ and _____.

Source: iStock.com/M-S-Night

During the unit, the students read books and engaged in activities to learn about plants and seeds. They learned about the food that we grow, the stages of growth from seed to plant, and what plants need to grow. This enhanced unit of study, based on anchor texts in the basal reading program, helped students gain knowledge and skills needed to meet the language arts and content science Standards. Through their involvement in this approach to language arts, all students, especially emergent bilingual students, became more proficient speakers, readers, and writers of English.

- Standards based skills: *create, summarize, recall, design*
- Content objective: *Students will describe how plants grow, what they need to grow, and the parts of plants.*
- Language objective: *Students will learn how to use and label illustrations to convey information.*

YOUR TURN: UNIT REFLECTION

BEFORE TEACHING THE UNIT, REFLECT ON THESE QUESTIONS:

1. Which of the strategies in the unit could you use with your students?
2. How might you modify the strategies for your context?
3. What additional activities might you add?
4. Considering your classroom schedule, how much time will you need to implement the strategies?

AFTER TEACHING THE UNIT, REFLECT ON THESE QUESTIONS:

1. Which of the strategies in the unit did you use?
2. Which activities were most successful with your students?
3. How did you modify the strategies?
4. What additional activities did you add?
5. How much time did you need to implement the strategies?

OUTLINE OF PLANTS AND SEEDS UNIT STRATEGIES

PREVIEW ACTIVITIES: DRAWING ON AND BUILDING BACKGROUND

Identifying Seeds

Looking at a large number of seeds in a picture or in a jar, students identify the ones they know. The teacher fills in a large circle graph with the names of the seeds students can identify.

- *Upper-grade students can work in groups to identify the seeds. They can refer to books showing different kinds of seeds and plants provided by the teacher.*

Circle Graph

Students in a group are given a plastic bag with a variety of seeds they have discussed. Each group is given a circle graph like the one the teacher filled in (see Figure 2.22). They glue the seeds in the circles on the graph and write the name of the seed under the seeds they have glued.

Figure 2.22   Circle Graph

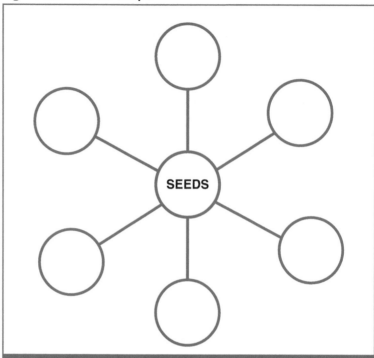

Classification of Seeds

Students working in groups fill in the classification chart using the seeds they have glued in the circles (see Figure 2.23). The teacher first completes one or two examples with the class and also reviews vocabulary of shapes and textures.

Figure 2.23   Classification of Seeds Chart

Kind of seed	Color of seed	Shape of seed	Texture: How does it feel?	Does it have an odor? Does it smell?

- *Upper-grade students can fill in the classification chart with a variety of seeds. Teachers should include seeds like acorns, walnuts, peas, avocado, apple, and seeds that fly, like dandelion seeds. The teacher may want to complete a couple of examples with the class first and review key descriptive words such as* smooth, sticky, odorless, *and* oblong.

Gallery Picture Walk

The teacher posts pictures of five plants around the classroom with a sheet of paper under each picture for students to write on. On a table, she puts seeds of each plant into five piles and numbers each pile. Working together, pairs of students identify the plants and match the picture of the plant with the number of one of the piles of seeds. They write a sentence under the picture to explain why they made their choice. After students have recorded their responses, they walk around the room again and read the answers their peers have written and discuss them.

- *For upper-grade students, the teacher first reads an upper-grade anchor book from the basal series about seeds* From Seed to Plant *(Gibbons, 1991) or some other grade-level appropriate book about seeds and plant growth to provide some background knowledge. Next, the teacher posts pictures of plants and seeds around the room with paper for comments. Ideally, there are pictures of plants like an oak tree and an acorn or a kernel of corn and a corn stalk so that students can identify that the acorn is the seed for the oak tree and the kernel is the seed for the corn stalk. Students are to identify the plants and seeds and make any written observation that they discuss with their partner. Class discussion should follow as students comment and ask questions.*

AS WE ENGAGE IN THE UNIT: VIEW ACTIVITIES

KWL Chart

Students brainstorm what they know and what they want to learn about seed and plant growth. The teacher records the students' comments using their words and puts the students' names next to their comments. As they gather information, they add it to the "What have we learned?" part of the chart (shown in Figure 2.24) in a different color. They cite the source of the new information.

Figure 2.24   KWL Chart

What do we know about plants and seeds?	What do we want to learn about plants and seeds?	What have we learned about plants and seeds?

- *Upper-grade students can do a turn and talk in pairs. Then pairs can go up and fill in the chart, writing their names by their contributions.*

Plant Growth Project

The students choose two or three different kinds of seeds and make pocket gardens with a plastic bag and seeds placed in paper towels dampened with water and a few drops of bleach. Seeds are placed in different environments: the sun, the dark, and the cold. Using template pages like Figure 2.25, students record their observations over time in journals they have assembled.

Figure 2.25   Template Pages for Student Journals

Date _____ How many days? _____ Was your seed in the sun, dark, or cold? _____ _____ Describe how the seed has changed. _____ _____ _____ _____ _____	Draw the seed. Show how the seed changes.

The teacher conducts a formative assessment using a rating scale (see Figure 2.26). The teacher explains how to use the scale and evaluates some sentences with the class. Next, students work in bilingual pairs to evaluate three sentences from their journal entries.

Figure 2.26   Rating Scale for Plant Journal

Name: _____

Did the student . . . ?	Not at all	Some of the time	Most of the time	All of the time
Write complete sentences				
Use past-tense verbs				
Use descriptive words				
Use ordinal numbers				

Picture Walk With Anchor Book:
Where Does Food Come From?

The teacher shows the students one of the anchor books from the basal program, *Where Does Food Come From?* (Rotner & Goss, 2006). Together the teacher and the students do a picture walk through the book. As they turn their pages, they identify what they see on each page and make comments about the different types of food.

The teacher reads the text to the students as they follow along, and then students read the book to each other in small groups. Students with the same home language may be grouped together to discuss the book using their home language or English. Next, students list the foods in the story and decide where the foods come from (see Figure 2.27).

Figure 2.27   **Where Do Foods Come From? Chart**

Food	Plant? Animal? Insect?	Name of plant, animal, or insect	Where do you find it? Farm? Forest? Garden?

The class discusses their answers, and each group adds information to their charts. Other books about food and where it comes from can be read and information from those books can be added to the chart.

- *Upper-grade students could be shown a large picture of a meal or read a book about a family having a special meal. It could be, for example, a Thanksgiving meal. They can work in groups or pairs and list the foods and where the foods come from. Class discussion should help answer any questions students might have.*

Translanguaging Venn Diagram

Read two books, one in Spanish (or another language) and one in English, that discuss plant growth, like *The Carrot Seed* (Krauss, 2004) and *Una semilla nada más* (*Just One Seed*; Ada, 1990). Have students compare and contrast the information about seeds and plant growth using a translanguaging Venn diagram like Figure 2.28.

Figure 2.28   Translanguaging Venn Diagram

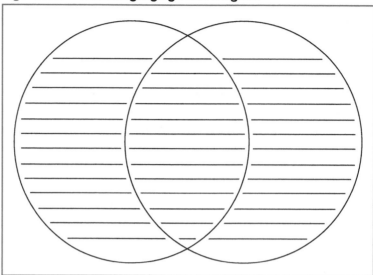

Turn and Talk and Review KWL Chart

After the class finishes the Venn diagram, the teacher asks the students to look back at their KWL charts and to tell her what they have learned so far about plants and seeds that is not already on the KWL chart. Students turn to a partner, and together the pair makes a list of what they have been learning that is not already on the chart and add it to the chart.

Parts of Plants We Eat

Bring to class various vegetables we eat, like cauliflower, a bunch of broccoli, an artichoke, some carrots, a bunch of beets, a bunch of radishes, a stalk of celery, some stalks of asparagus, a cucumber, some cherry tomatoes, a head of cabbage, a head of lettuce, and a bunch of spinach. After identifying the vegetables with the class, show them a large sheet of butcher paper with a huge flowering plant on it. Label the parts of the plant on the drawing. Then ask the class to help you put the vegetables that are flowers on the flower, those that are stems on the stem, those that are roots on the root, and those that are leaves on the leaves.

- *Upper-grade students who have read* From Seeds to Plants *(Gibbons, 1991) or* The Reason for a Flower: A Book About Flowers, Pollen, and Seeds *(Heller, 1999) can draw and label the parts of a flower, including the anther, filament, stamen, pistil, stigma, style, and ovule.*

Students write two sentences, one telling three vegetables they like, and the other telling three they dislike. The teacher uses a rating scale like Figure 2.29 to evaluate students' use of commas in the sentences.

Figure 2.29   Rating Scale for Commas in List

Name	Did not use commas correctly	Used commas correctly some of the time	Used commas correctly most of the time	Used commas correctly all of the time

Predicting Vocabulary With Anchor Book

Students look at the cover of one of the program's anchor books for a unit and read the title. Next, the teacher asks the students to think about what they know about the topic and the books they have already read about the topic. Students then predict some words they think they will find when they read the text. Students first turn to a partner and talk together about some words, and then the whole class shares. As the teacher reads the book, students raise their hands when they hear one of the words they had predicted.

- *Upper-grade students can predict flower vocabulary they already know, including names of flowers, from the basal anchor book, A Spring Walk (Snow, 2015). They can then discuss what they know about the flowers they recognize.*

Sequence Stages of Growth Chart: *From Seed to Pumpkin*

The teacher gives the students a sequence chart to draw and label the growth stages of the pumpkin (see Figure 2.30). Students read through the story and in pairs fill in the boxes on the chart by drawing and labeling in order of growth: seed, seedling, leaves, vine, bud, flower, small green pumpkin, and large orange pumpkin. The teacher brainstorms a list of signal words showing time sequence. Then the teacher and students write a paragraph about plant growth using the sequence chart and the list of signal words.

Figure 2.30   Sequence Chart

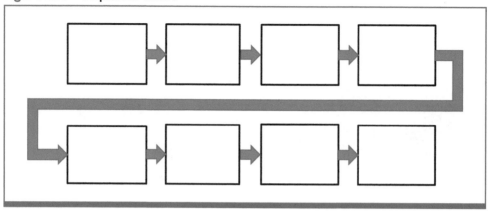

- *Upper-grade students who have read books like* From Seeds to Plants *or* The Reason for a Flower: A Book About Flowers, Pollen, and Seeds *can draw and label how flowers are pollinated.*

Celery-Stalk Root Absorption Activity

The teacher brings glass or clear plastic jars, a food-coloring kit, and some celery stalks with leaves to class. Students choose colors from the food coloring kit to color the water in the jars. They put the celery stalks in the water. They check each day to see if the stalks absorb the colored water. They record results on a sheet (see Figure 2.31), writing their observations and drawing and coloring what they notice each day.

Figure 2.31   Celery Experiment Record Sheet

Day 1	Draw and color.	What did you observe?
Day 2	Draw and color.	What did you observe?
Day 3	Draw and color.	What did you observe?
Day 4	Draw and color.	What did you observe?

- *Upper-grade students who have read books like* From Seeds to Plants *or* The Reason for a Flower *should list the many ways seeds are distributed by weather and/or by people or animals.*

REVIEW ACTIVITIES FOR PLANTS AND SEEDS UNIT

Measure and Graph Plants

Students transplant seedlings from their pocket gardens to soil in plastic cups. They measure the plant growth and record it in their journals (see Figure 2.32).

Figure 2.32   Stem and Root Graph

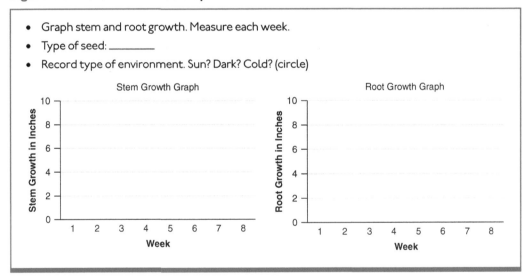

- Graph stem and root growth. Measure each week.
- Type of seed: _____
- Record type of environment. Sun? Dark? Cold? (circle)

- *Upper-grade students can dissect a large flower and locate the various parts of the flower. They can draw each part and label it. They can also draw a picture, label it, and describe photosynthesis.*

Write a Procedure

The teacher works with the class to write a paragraph recounting the steps they took during the seeds, plants, and plant growth unit. Then she has the class convert the paragraph into a numbered list. Students find differences between the paragraph and the numbered list, and the teacher explains that the list is in the form of a science procedure.

Science Procedure

1. Choose three kinds of seeds.
2. Moisten a paper towel with water mixed with a little bleach.
3. Place the seeds in the towel.
4. Place the seeds and the towel in a plastic bag.
5. Place the plastic bag in the sun (or in a dark place, or in a cold place).
6. Observe the seed three times a week.
7. Record and draw the changes you see in the seeds in your seed journal.
8. Draw conclusions based on your observations.

All About Plants Book

The teacher and the students use iPads to take pictures of their activities during the plant growth unit, and in pairs students create their own *All About Plants* book, inserting pictures in the pages and including text that explains the parts of plants and what plants need.

- *Upper-grade students can write a report describing how plants are pollinated or how seeds are dispersed and new plants grow from seeds.*

BASAL ANCHOR BOOKS FOR THE UNIT

Gibbons, G. (1991). *From seeds to plants*. Carmel, CA: Hampton-Brown Books.

Pfeffer, W. (2015). *From seed to pumpkin*. New York, NY: HarperCollins.

Rotner, S., & Goss, G. (2006). *Where does food come from?* Minneapolis, MN: Millbrook.

Snow, V. B. (2015). *Spring walk*. Salt Lake City, UT: Gibbs Smith.

SUPPLEMENTAL PLANT BOOKS IN SPANISH AND ENGLISH

Ada, A. F. (1990). *Una semilla nada más*. Carmel, CA: Hampton-Brown.

Bolton, F., & Snowball, D. (1985). *Growing radishes and carrots*. New York, NY: Scholastic.

Butterworth, C. (2013). *How did that get into my lunchbox? The story of food*. Somerworth, MA: Candlewick.

Castor, D. (2009). *What do plants need?* Pelham, NY: Benchmark Education.

Cerier, L. (n.d.). *The three sisters*. Boston, MA: Houghton Mifflin.

Cole, J. (1995). *El autobús mágico planta una semilla*. New York, NY: Scholastic.

Cory Lindquist, R. (1997). *Grandma Carol's plants*. Crystal Lake, IL: Rigby.

Creasy, M.-A. (2012). *What's for breakfast?* Temecula, CA: Okapi.

Creasy, M.-A. (2015). *¿Qué hay para desayunar?* Temecula, CA: Okapi.

Cutting, B., & Cutting, J. (1995). *Semillas y más semillas* (G. Andujar, Trans.). Bothell, WA: Wright Group.

Flint, D. (1998). *Where does breakfast come from?* Crystal Lake, IL: Rigby.

Flores, G. S. (1985). *Pon una semilla a germinar*. México, D.F.: Editorial Trillas.

Gibbons, G. (1991). *From seeds to plants*. Carmel, CA: Hampton-Brown.

Heller, R. (1983a). *La razón de ser de una flor*. New York, NY: Scholastic.

Heller, R. (1983b). *The reason for a flower*. New York, NY: Scholastic.

Heller, R. (1999). *The reason for a flower: A book about flowers, pollen, and seeds*. New York, NY: Penguin Putnam Books for Young Readers.

Hughes, M. (1993). *Un puñado de semillas*. Caracas, Venezuela: Ediciones Ekaré.

Jordan, H. J. (1996). *Cómo crece una semilla* (M. A. Fiol, Trans.). New York, NY: HarperCollins.

Kalman, B. (1997). *How a plant grows*. New York, NY: Crabtree .

Kalman, B. (2005). *Photosynthesis: Changing sunlight into food*. New York, NY: Crabtree.

Kalman, B. (2007). *Plants are living things*. New York, NY: Crabtree.

Kaiman, B. (2011). *Where does our food come from?* New York, NY: Crabtree.

Kratky, L. (1995). *¿Qué sale de las semillas?* Carmel, CA: Hampton-Brown.

Krauss, R. (1945). *The carrot seed*. New York, NY: Scholastic.

Krauss, R. (1945, 1978 trans.). *La semilla de zanahoria* (A. Palacios, Trans.). New York, NY: Scholastic.

Krauss, R. (1996). *La semilla de zanahoria* (A. Palacios, Trans.). New York, NY: Scholastic.

Krauss, R. (2004). *The carrot seed*. New York, NY: Harper Trophy.

Lindeen, M. (2018). *What plants need*. Chicago, IL: Norwood House.

Lucca, M. (2001). *Plants grow from seeds*. Washington, DC: National Geographic Society.

Lucca, M. (2003). *De las semillas nacen las plantas*. Washington, DC: National Geographic Society.

Marzollo, J. (1996). *I'm a seed*. Carmel, CA: Hampton Brown.

McQueen, L. (1985). *The little red hen*. New York, NY: Scholastic.

Pfeffer, W. (2015). *From seed to pumpkin*. New York, NY: HarperCollins.

Rotner, S., & Goss, G. (2006). *Where does food come from?* Minneapolis, MN: Millbrook.

Schultz, S. (n.d.). *The flower*. Boston, MA: Houghton Mifflin Harcourt.

Shanahan, K. (2014). *The great pumpkin-growing contest*. Temecula, CA: Okapi.

Shanahan, K. (2019). *How do plants survive?* Temecula, CA: Okapi.

Shulman, L. (2004). *Plants we use*. Barrington, IL: Rigby.

Snow, V. B. (2015). *Spring walk*. Salt Lake City, UT: Gibbs Smith.

Solano Flores, G. (1988). *Pon una semilla a germinar*. México, D.F.: Editorial Trillas.

Spilsbury, L., & Spilsbury, R. (2005). *Where do plants grow?* Mankato, MN: Heinemann.

Stilwel, D. (2012). *Where does our food come from?* Milwaukee, WI: Gareth Stevens.

Walker, C. (1992a). *Plants and seeds*. Bothell, WA: The Wright Group.

Walker, C. (1992b). *Seeds grow*. Bothell, WA: The Wright Group.

Walker, C. (1993a). *Different plants, different places*. Cleveland, OH: Simon & Schuster.

Walker, C. (1993b). *Edible plants*. Cleveland, OH: Simon & Schuster.

Walker, C. (1993c). *How plants live and grow*. Cleveland, OH: Simon & Schuster.

Walker, C. (1995a). *Las semillas crecen* (G. Andujar, Trans.). Bothell, WA: Wright Group.

Walker, C. (1995b). *Plantas y semillas* (G. Andujar, Trans.). Bothell, WA: Wright Group.

CHAPTER THREE

Making the Input Comprehensible

A Habitats Unit

In this chapter, we provide readers with a specific, step-by-step description of an upper-grade unit on habitats, a unit commonly taught in basal and alternative comprehensive literacy programs. We begin by discussing the importance of making the input comprehensible and then show how a teacher planned strategies to make the instructional input comprehensible during the unit.

MAKING THE INPUT COMPREHENSIBLE

Krashen (1982) developed the monitor model for second language acquisition. His theory has been the basis for the teaching of English learners in many elementary and secondary classes. A key hypothesis of this theory is his argument that *comprehensible input* is the key to second language acquisition. Krashen explains that we cannot learn what we don't understand, and that teachers should make anything they teach their emergent bilinguals comprehensible. When we receive messages, oral or written, that we understand, we acquire proficiency in a language.

In Figure 3.1 we list several techniques for making the input comprehensible. We suggest teachers use these strategies for teaching both native English speakers and English learners.

Figure 3.1   **Making the Input Comprehensible**

- Use visuals and realia (real things). Always try to move from the concrete to the abstract.

- Use videos and DVDs.

- Use gestures and body language.

- Speak clearly and pause often, but don't slow speech down unnaturally.

- Say the same thing in different ways (paraphrase).

- Write key words and ideas down. This slows down the language for English learners.

- Use current technology to project relevant material whenever appropriate.

- Make frequent comprehension checks.

- Keep oral presentations or reading assignments short.

- Organize collaborative activities, as they are more effective than lectures or assigned readings.

- Have students explain main concepts to one another working in pairs (turn and talk) or small groups. Emergent bilinguals can use their home language to do this.

- Allow emergent bilinguals to write down what they understand in their home language before writing or explaining orally in English.

Home Language Supports for Comprehensible Input

Our last two suggestions include use of students' home languages. If students enter school speaking languages other than English, and if English is the only language of instruction, then the students may simply not understand enough English to acquire the language or to learn the content taught in the language. Emergent bilinguals may find much of the English instruction incomprehensible. The use of the first language to help make the second language understandable and accessible is often the most efficient way to help students acquire the second language.

Although delivering instruction in the home language may not be possible in the English language arts classroom for a variety of reasons, teachers in monolingual English teaching settings can find ways to use their emergent bilingual students' home languages to promote academic success. In Figure 3.2 we suggest a list of additional ideas for using the home language to make the input comprehensible.

Figure 3.2   Using the Home Language to Make the Input Comprehensible

- Ensure that some of the environmental print in the classroom reflects students' first languages.

- Supply school and classroom libraries with books, magazines, and other resources in students' home languages.

- Allow emergent bilinguals to read and write with aides and other students who speak their first language.

- Encourage students to publish books and other writing and share their stories in languages other than English or produce bilingual books in English and the students' home languages.

- Allow emergent bilinguals to respond in their home languages to demonstrate comprehension of content taught in English.

- Use DVDs or video clips in languages other than English to support academic learning.

As we describe the unit on habitats that follows, we include different strategies that make the input comprehensible, including some that support the use of students' home languages.

PUTTING THE UNIT INTO CONTEXT: ROBERT'S UNIT ON HABITATS

Robert is a student teacher in an upper elementary classroom in a school in California. His district requires that all teachers use the district-adopted basal reading program to teach reading because the materials are connected to Standards and include assessments that help the district report student data. The basal reader is organized around units of inquiry and includes both literature and informational text selections.

The students in Robert's classroom come from different cultural backgrounds, and many are bilingual, although all appear to speak and understand English. There is a world map in the classroom indicating where students or their parents or grandparents come from (see Chapter 1). Robert knows that many of his students or their parents have roots in Asia, Mexico, Central America, the Middle East, or South America. After working with these students for a couple of months, Robert realizes that not all students are able to understand or respond adequately to the basal materials.

He has conducted a variety of activities to get to know his English learners, another of the overarching principles for effective teaching. He has reviewed their cumulative folders and conducted an on-demand writing assessment. He has also taken anecdotal notes on their oral English proficiency as they speak and on their reading ability. With this information, he has classified his emergent bilinguals as newly arrived with adequate schooling, newly arrived with limited formal schooling, or potential long-term English learners. He has used this information to determine the language proficiency of his English learners based on his state's language proficiency levels.

Robert is taking a class at his university on ESL methodology. His solo teaching assignment in the English language arts class requires him to teach a unit from the basal program. The class where he is student teaching is working on readings from the basal on habitats. Robert wants to try to make the unit comprehensible and accessible to all his students, including those who are emergent bilinguals. With the help of his university professor and his master teacher, Robert organizes the unit with activities that engage the students and help them participate fully in the basal reading materials. Robert decides that a big question for this unit is, "What are the characteristics of different habitats and what animals and plants live in these habitats?" Organizing around units of inquiry based on big questions is one of the overarching principles for effective language teaching. The first activities are designed to preview the unit. The next activities—the view activities—are carried out as students engage in the unit activities. The unit review activities help reinforce the main concepts from the unit, as well as the language structures and vocabulary used in the unit.

PREVIEW ACTIVITIES: DRAWING ON AND BUILDING BACKGROUND

Observation Charts

To build background for this unit of study, Robert collects pictures of various animal habitats from the library, magazines, and the Internet. He posts pictures of the desert, the ocean, a coral reef, a rainforest, a deciduous forest, a grassland, and the arctic around the classroom (see Figure 3.3). Below each picture he posts a sheet a paper. Robert asks his students to work with a partner. Students with less English proficiency are encouraged to partner with a native English speaker or with a student who speaks their home language. He gives each pair only one pencil and tells them to talk about the pictures. Working together, each pair is to write on the paper under each picture (1) an observation, (2) a question, (3) a comment, and (4) a connection.

To help his students write questions, Robert teaches a mini-lesson on *wh-* questions. He asks students for words beginning with *wh-* that start a question. They respond with the different *wh-* words, *what, when, where,* and *why?* He points out that other questions start with *how*, a word that contains a *w* and an *h*. Then he has pairs of students write questions about their school. As they report back, he writes their questions on the board. He points out that each question starts with one of the *wh-* words and ends with a question mark. He also notes that the word that follows the *wh-* word is a verb. He leaves their questions on the board so that the students can refer to them as they write their questions about habitats.

Robert begins by modeling how he would respond to the desert habitat picture. Then he brainstorms additional observations, questions, comments, and connections with the whole class. He adds these to the desert sheet. After each pair moves around the room and responds to the other habitat pictures, Robert asks students to walk around the room again and read their classmates' comments.

This activity provides different kinds of comprehensible input to Robert's emergent bilingual students. The pictures give students important visual information for the activity; his mini-lesson on *wh-* questions helps students write their questions; his modeling helps students understand what to do as they move around the room; and as students work in pairs, they receive support from their classmates. Students working with a home-language partner are able to talk about the pictures in their home languages and help each other report back to the class in English.

Robert further helps his English learners make sense of the content by leaving the pictures and sheets up for several days and encouraging students to return to them and add additional observations, questions, comments, or connections. Robert uses these comments and questions to assess his students' background knowledge.

Figure 3.3   Habitat Pictures

desert	**ocean**	**coral reef**
Source: Pixabay.com/falkenpost	*Source:* Pixabay.com/joakant	*Source:* Pixabay.com/ dimitrisvetsikas1969
rainforest	**deciduous forest**	**grassland**
Source: Pixabay.com/mrsbrown	*Source:* Pixabay.com/congerdesign	*Source:* Pixabay.com/12019
	arctic	
	Source: Pixabay.com/girlart39	

- Standards based skills: *draw on background knowledge, make connections, ask probing questions*
- Content objective: *Students will recognize that there are differences among habitats.*
- Language objective: *Students will be able to form* wh- *questions.*

VIDEO

Robert follows this introductory activity with a video about habitats he finds on YouTube. Using video clips is one way Robert makes academic content comprehensible for his students. He notes there are many videos to choose from, and he chooses one especially for kids that is appropriate for his upper-grade students. After showing the video, he asks students to do a turn and talk to discuss what they learned about habitats by viewing the video. When both students in a pair speak the same home language, they can choose to talk in either their home language or in English. This translanguaging strategy is another way Robert makes input comprehensible.

- Standards based skills: *build background knowledge, make connections*

KWL CHART

Next, the class begins a KWL chart (Figure 3.4). Robert asks students, "What do we know about habitats?" and "What do we want to know about habitats?" Through this activity, Robert draws on his students' background knowledge, another of the overarching principles for teaching English learners. He records the students' comments using their words and writes students' names next to their comments.

Writing down the students' ideas in front of them helps his emergent bilinguals develop language and helps them understand the content they are studying. As the unit progresses, the class returns to the chart using different-colored markers each time they write new information. Students also are asked to give the source of the new information they add under the "What have we learned?" section of the chart. To help his students form complex sentences, Robert writes a sentence frame on the board: "We have learned that _____."

When they finish the unit, they come back to the chart to fill in the What Have We Learned? section. All of these preview activities help students build the background knowledge and the vocabulary they need to read the different texts in the basal unit.

Figure 3.4   KWL Chart

What do we know about habitats?	What do we want to know about habitats?	What have we learned about habitats?

- Standards based skills: *draw on background knowledge, explain*
- Content objective: *Students will add to their knowledge about habitats.*
- Language objective: *Students will produce complex sentences with embedded clauses beginning with "that." ("We know that camels live in desert habitats.")*

AS WE ENGAGE IN THE UNIT: VIEW ACTIVITIES

As We Are Learning Chart

The class then begins a new chart, As We Are Learning (see Figure 3.5). This chart, like the KWL chart, is displayed in the classroom throughout the unit. As students learn about different habitats, they fill in information about each, listing the animal life in the habitat, the plant life in the habitat, and vocabulary related to this habitat. The teacher or the students can also find an image of the habitat on the Internet and add it to the chart.

Figure 3.5   As We Are Learning Chart

Habitat	Image	Animal Life	Plant Life	Vocabulary

- Standards based skills: *draw on background knowledge, describe*
- Content objective: *Students will identify the different animals and plants that live in various habitats.*

- Language objective: *Students will identify key vocabulary related to each habitat.*

Multilingual Word Wall

After viewing the video and sharing ideas, the students are able to list various vocabulary words related to habitats. Using these lists, Robert and his students create a multilingual word wall (see Figure 3.6). Using multilingual cognate word walls is an effective way Robert creates a multilingual/multicultural environment, another of the overarching principles for effective teaching.

On this chart, students who speak a language other than English can write down the key words in their languages. If they don't know the words, Robert encourages them to ask their parents or look online. Several students who speak a non-alphabetic language are excited to look online and copy the words, as only a few can write in their home language. This translanguaging strategy makes the academic content more comprehensible for his emergent bilingual students. Spanish speakers note how many words in Spanish look like English words, and Robert explains that these are called cognates and that noticing cognates can help them understand the English they are reading. Robert's classroom chart looks something like the following:

Figure 3.6 Multilingual Word Wall

Habitat words English	Habitat words Spanish	Habitat words Tagalog	Habitat words Mandarin	Habitat words Arabic	Habitat words Korean
habitat	habitat	tirahan	栖息地	موطن	서식지
desert	desierto	disyerto	沙漠	صحراء	사막
forest	bosque	kagubatan	森林	غابة	숲
ocean	océano	karagatan	海洋	محيط	대양
environment	ambiente	kapaligiran	环境	بيئة	환경
adaptation	adaptación	pagbagay	适应	تكيف	적응
survive	sobrevivir	mabuhay	生存	ينجو	생존하다

- Standards based skills: *compare and contrast, draw on background knowledge*

- Content objective: *Students will learn the academic vocabulary related to habitats.*
- Language objective: *Students will develop the concept of cognates and begin to use cognates as they read.*

TURN AND TALK

The first reading from the basal Robert's class uses is *A Walk in the Desert* (Arnold, 1990). Before reading the excerpt, as a prereading activity, Robert has the students do a turn and talk. He asks the following questions:

- What do you know about the desert?
- Have you been to a desert? What do you remember about it?
- Would you prefer to live here or in a desert? Why?

Again, he encourages students with the same home language to use their home language as they discuss these questions, using another effective translanguaging strategy. Students then share as a whole group what they discussed in their pairs. As they report orally, Robert reminds them that they can tell *Why* by using a sentence with *because*.

- Standards based skills: *draw on background knowledge, explain, summarize*
- Content objective: *Students will learn new characteristics of a desert environment.*
- Language objective: *Students will form complex sentences using signal words showing cause. ("I prefer to live here* because *the desert is so hot and dry.")*

Since several of Robert's students would have difficulty reading the basal text independently, he decides to begin with a read aloud. He reads the *Walk in the Desert,* stopping frequently to comment, to point to pictures, or to ask students to comment. Read alouds help make the reading input comprehensible for his emergent bilinguals. Robert uses the different stages of the gradual release of responsibility model to help his students develop English reading proficiency. For example, later he has his students engage in interactive reading of a story selection, pairing his emergent bilinguals with students whose home language is English. The gradual release model is another of the key practices for working with English learners.

After Robert reads the selection, the class fills in the As We Are Learning chart for the habitat—the desert—drawing on the text to fill in the information (see Figure 3.7).

Figure 3.7 As We Are Learning Desert Chart

Habitat	Image	Animal Life	Plant Life	Vocabulary Related to Habitat
Desert	*Source:* Pixabay.com/falkenpost			

Figure 3.8 Multilingual Word Wall Desert

Desert words English	Desert words Spanish	Desert words Tagalog	Desert words Mandarin	Desert words Arabic	Desert words Korean

After that, Robert has the students take the vocabulary they identified related to their desert reading and add the words to their multilingual word wall (see Figure 3.8).

Spanish-speaking students identify cognates on their list of words, including *clima* for *climate*, *cactus* or *cacto* for *cactus*, *espinas* for *spines*, and *gigante* for *giant*. They also note that *saguaro*, a type of cactus, is the same word in Spanish and English.

As a follow-up activity, Robert offers the students a choice of the following assignments.

1. You have just spent a day walking in the desert. Write a *diary entry* telling about what you saw. Get ideas for your entry from *A Walk in the Desert*. Use new vocabulary words you have learned from the story.
2. From the point of view of an animal living in the desert, write a diary entry describing your day. Include interactions you have with other animals and plants. Use new vocabulary words you have learned from the story.

3. Write an *adventure story* from the point of view of an animal or bird from *A Walk in the Desert*. Include other animals and plants from *A Walk in the Desert* in your story.

After the students have finished writing, Robert has students use a self-assessment checklist he has created to do a quick formative assessment of their writing skills and their inclusion of the new vocabulary. Robert reviews these checklists to plan a follow-up lesson that gives students more opportunity to write and use vocabulary they have learned. Figure 3.9 shows the checklist.

Figure 3.9   Self-Assessment Checklist

Name: _____

Did I . . . ?	Yes	No
Use first person pronouns (I, me, my)		
Write complete sentences		
Begin sentences with a capital letter and end with a period, question mark, or exclamation point		
Use desert vocabulary that I have learned		

- Standards based skills: *create, infer/predict, point of view, genre: narrative, diary, or fictional narrative*
- Content objective: *Students will be able to include key information about the desert habitat.*
- Language objective: *Students will use the structure of a diary entry or of a narrative as they write. Students will use vocabulary related to the desert.*

The basal anchor reading that follows is a fiction book set in the desert, *Roadrunner's Dance* by Rodolfo Anaya (Anaya & Diaz, 2000). Before they read the story, Robert asks students to turn and talk to a partner, answering the following question: Tell about a time you had a problem and someone helped you. Robert asks students to think about how their experience relates to the story as they read it.

SAY SOMETHING

Robert has his students read the story interactively, working in pairs. Structuring this as a collaborative activity helps make the input more comprehensible. Students take turns reading the pages. After the students read a page, they stop and *say something*. Robert has taught them that a *say something* can be a comment, a question, a prediction, or a connection between the reading and their own experience. After the interactive pair reading and the *say somethings*, students again add to the As We Are Learning chart. This time, they add details to the desert section of the chart.

- <u>Standards based skills:</u> *predict, make a connection, draw on background knowledge, make a personal connection*
- <u>Content objective:</u> *Students will draw on what they are learning about the desert and make a personal connection.*
- <u>Language objective:</u> *Students use the future tense in their predictions of what will happen, and they use the "same as" structures for connections.*

POST-IT NOTE READING ACTIVITY

The next anchor text reading for the unit on habitats in the basal is a section from John Muir's *Our National Parks* (Muir, 2017). Robert knows that a skill students need to develop is to distinguish between main ideas and details in their reading. He gives the students Post-it notes and tells them they will read the excerpt independently. As they read, they are to write on a Post-it one main idea and some related details from each page. Robert tells his emergent bilinguals they can write their notes in English or in their home language. Because students have not done this before, Robert and the students do it together for the first two pages. Then students continue to read independently, identifying main ideas and details.

Once students complete their reading and their Post-its, Robert puts them in small groups. Using their notes, students share what they think are the main ideas for each page. Robert asks students to come to a consensus if they differ and then share the main ideas they identified. The students in each group also make a list of vocabulary words they note related to national parks. As a final activity, with Robert as the scribe, the class makes a master list of these vocabulary words to post in the classroom. The students share the main ideas for each page, the details they found, and the vocabulary they identified. They also include the new vocabulary in their multilingual word wall (see Figure 3.10).

Figure 3.10   Multilingual Word Wall: Parks

Parks words English	Parks words Spanish	Parks words Tagalog	Parks words Mandarin	Parks words Arabic	Parks words Korean

Writing key words and ideas on charts, such as the KWL chart or the As We Are Learning chart, is another way Robert makes academic input more comprehensible for his emergent bilinguals.

- Standards based skill: *identify main ideas and supporting details*
- Content objective: *Students understand the role of national parks in preserving different habitats.*
- Language objective: *Students learn content-specific academic vocabulary.*

YOU BE THE TEACHER JIGSAW AND GALLERY WALK

Robert uses a type of jigsaw activity known as You Be the Teacher to help students access and engage in the next habitat reading from the basal, *At Home in the Coral Reef* (Muzik & Brown-Wing, 1995). He forms groups of four to five students. Each group is given two to three pages from the selection to read. Then each group makes a poster that includes:

- A drawing to represent their section
- The main idea and at least one supporting detail from each page
- New words they have learned about the coral reef

Collaborative activities such as this one make the input more comprehensible. When they finish, each student in the group initials his/her contribution to the poster. Then the groups put up their posters around the classroom.

- Standards based skills: *identify main idea and details, analyze, display information with an image*
- Content objective: *Students will be able to describe a coral reef habitat.*
- Language objective: *Students will use content-specific academic vocabulary related to coral reefs.*

Next, students in each group number off and move to form new groups. All the number ones are in one group, all the twos are in another, and so forth. The groups then do a gallery walk. At each poster, the students who helped make that poster explain why they chose the information they included.

- Standards based skills: *describe/explain orally*
- Content objective: *Students will learn key ideas about a coral reef habitat.*
- Language objective: *Students will explain using sentences with cause signal words: "We drew this picture because . . ." "We decided the main idea was because . . .".*

Robert and the class now add the information they have learned about the coral reefs habitat to the As We Are Learning chart (see Figure 3.11).

Figure 3.11   **As We Are Learning Chart: Coral Reefs**

Habitat	Image	Animal Life	Plant Life	Vocabulary
Desert	*Source:* Pixabay.com/falkenpost			
Coral Reefs	*Source:* Pixabay.com/joakant			

The final anchor book related to the habitat unit in the basal reading program is the narrative nonfiction text *Adelina's Whales* (Sobol, 2003). This story explains the migration patterns of gray whales and is written in story form. Before reading, Robert asks students to turn and talk to a partner, answering the following questions:

- What do you know about whales?
- Have you ever seen a whale?
- What do you know about a whale's habitat?

Emergent bilinguals in the class can use their home language during the turn and talk. Next, the class discusses their answers, and Robert uses this information to create another KWL chart, this one about whales.

STORY MAP/STORY BOARD

Robert then projects a story map on the classroom whiteboard (see Figure 3.12). The students read *Adelina's Whales* independently. After this, Robert guides the students as they fill in the story map. They identify characters and setting as well as sequences of events that occur as the whales migrate. After they finish the story map, Robert reads aloud some sections containing vivid descriptions of the setting and the characters. Then he has students write about the setting of the story or one of the characters using descriptive adjectives.

Figure 3.12   Story Map

Title		Author
Setting		Characters
Beginning	Middle	End

- Standards based skills: *order of events, create, summarize, describe*
- Content objective: *Students identify story elements.*
- Language objective: *Students use descriptive adjectives in their writing.*

Figure 3.13   As We Are Learning Chart: Oceans

Habitat	Image	Animal Life	Plant Life	Vocabulary
Desert	*Source:* Pixabay.com/falkenpost			
Coral Reefs	*Source:* Pixabay.com/joakant			
Oceans	*Source:* Pixabay.com/dimitrisvetsikas1969			

Figure 3.14   Multilingual Word Wall: Oceans

Ocean words English	Ocean words Spanish	Ocean words Tagalog	Ocean words Mandarin	Ocean words Arabic	Ocean words Korean

After reading *Adelina's Whales,* students add information about the ocean habitat for whales to the As We Are Learning chart (see Figure 3.13).

Drawing on the As We Are Learning chart for both coral reefs and oceans, Robert and his students add more key vocabulary words to their multilingual word wall (Figure 3.14).

REVIEW ACTIVITIES FOR HABITATS UNIT

The final project Robert has planned for the unit is an individual, partner, or group project. Students are to create a travel brochure for a place in a habitat that interests them or they have visited. The students use the information they learned as they studied different habitats. For example, they may write about places people visit like the Grand Canyon, Humboldt Redwoods State Park, Carlsbad Caverns, Yellowstone National Park, the Everglades, the Amazon Rainforest, the Great Barrier Reef, or the African Savanna. Robert encourages the students to conduct Internet searches for further information on the habitat they have chosen, and he provides extra books he has found in the school library. We have provided a bibliography of books on habitats in English and Spanish at the end of this chapter. Using their As We Are Learning chart and the readings, he asks students to include the information below in their brochures. He encourages bilingual students to include some information in their brochure in their home language.

- Pictures
- Description of the place
- Animals you will see
- Plants you will see
- Activities you can do there
- Why this is a great place to visit. Convince me I should go there.

To help his students include persuasive language in the section of their brochure designed to convince someone to visit that place, Robert makes a list of words on the board. The list includes *might, should, must, could,* and *ought to.* Then he asks students to work in pairs to put this list in a sequence from polite to most persuasive. When they finish, he leads a discussion of the order they have decided on, and he asks them if they can think of other words to add. One student suggests the phrase "absolutely must." Robert leaves the list up for students to use as they write their brochures.

Robert passes out a rubric he has created to evaluate the brochures (see Figure 3.15). He explains students should use it to be sure they have

Figure 3.15   Robert's Brochure Rubric

Name: _____

Does not have pictures	Has one picture	Has two pictures	Has three or more pictures
Has very little description of the place	Has some details to describe the place	Has quite a few details to describe the place	Has many details to describe the place
Does not name an animal found here	Names one animal found here	Names two animals found here	Names three or more animals found here
Does not name a plant found here	Names one plant found here	Names two plants found here	Names three or more plants found here
Does not name an activity that is done here	Names one activity that is done here	Names two activities that are done here	Names three or more activities that are done here
Does not list why this is a great place	Lists one reason this is a great place	Lists two reasons this is a great place	Lists three or more reasons this is a great place

met all the requirements. This helps the students understand exactly what Robert will be looking for in their finished brochures. Robert also explains he plans to have his class share their brochures with students from other classes and with parents during a back-to-school night. In this way, he ensures that his students have an audience for their writing.

During this unit, Robert supported students at different levels of English proficiency and helped them access and become engaged with the mandated reading materials. He taught them language arts skills and reading strategies, and he involved them in oral and written language.

- Standards based skills: *create, summarize, recall, design, persuade*
- Content objective: *Students will describe habitats and identify the animals and plants in the habitat.*
- Language objective: *Students will use persuasive language including modals such as* should, must, *and* ought to *as they design the brochure.*

YOUR TURN: UNIT REFLECTION

BEFORE TEACHING THE UNIT, REFLECT ON THESE QUESTIONS:

1. Which of the strategies in the unit could you use with your students?

2. How might you modify the strategies for your context?

3. What additional activities might you add?

4. Considering your classroom schedule, how much time will you need to implement the strategies?

AFTER TEACHING THE UNIT, REFLECT ON THESE QUESTIONS:

1. Which of the strategies in the unit did you use?

2. Which activities were most successful with your students?

3. How did you modify the strategies?

4. What additional activities did you add?

5. How much time did you need to implement the strategies?

OUTLINE OF HABITATS UNIT STRATEGIES

PREVIEW ACTIVITIES: DRAWING ON AND BUILDING BACKGROUND

Observation Charts

Put pictures of habitats around the room. Pairs write an observation, a question, a comment, or a connection on a sheet of paper under the pictures. They add to their observations, questions, comments, and connections during the unit. To help students write questions, the teacher teaches a mini-lesson on *wh-* questions.

- *Lower-grade students can work in pairs to label pictures around the room with words they know. The teacher can follow up by discussing the pictures and their contributions and adding to what they have written. Alternatively, younger students could be given descriptive words on Post-its and work with partners to walk around the room and post the adjectives under the habitats they think they represent. Some of the words they could be given include* warm, cold, dry, green, brown, *etc.*

YouTube Video on Habitats

Show students a video appropriate for their age group. Students to do a turn and talk to discuss what they learned about habitats by viewing the video.

KWL Chart

Students brainstorm what they know and what they want to know about habitats (see Figure 3.16). As they gather information, they add it to the "What have we learned?" part of the chart in a different color. They cite the source of the new information. The teacher gives students a sentence frame to help them write complex sentences: "We have learned that _____."

Figure 3.16   KWL Chart

What do we know about habitats?	What do we want to know about habitats?	What have we learned about habitats?

- *In lower grades, students can be put into groups and each group assigned a habitat. As a group, they brainstorm what they know and what they want to know about that habitat. From there, the teacher records as each group shares out. Once the teacher does the writing that students are not yet able to do themselves, the class reads what is written together.*

AS WE ENGAGE IN THE UNIT: VIEW ACTIVITIES

As We Are Learning Chart

Make an As We Are Learning chart (see Figure 3.17) to record information as students read about different habitats.

- *In lower grades, students could be put into groups and brainstorm the description, animal life, plant life, or vocabulary. Each group shares out as teacher records. Students and the teacher then read all the orally shared ideas together.*

Figure 3.17   As We Are Learning Chart

Habitat	Image	Animal Life	Plant Life	Vocabulary

Multilingual Word Wall

Develop a chart key with vocabulary in the home languages of emergent bilingual students (see Figure 3.18). Display in the room throughout the unit. Teach about cognates for languages with cognates.

Figure 3.18   Multilingual Word Wall

Habitat words English	Habitat words Spanish	Habitat words Tagalog	Habitat words Mandarin	Habitat words Arabic	Habitat words Korean

From *A Walk in the Desert* Prereading Activities

TURN AND TALK

Have students work in pairs to discuss the following questions. Remind them that they can explain "why" by using sentences with "because."

- What do you know about the desert?
- Have you been to a desert? What do you remember about it?
- Would you prefer to live here or in a desert? Why?

AS WE ARE LEARNING CHART: DESERT

After reading the story, have the class fill in information on the As We Are Learning: Desert chart (see Figure 3.19).

MULTILINGUAL WORD WALL: DESERT

Have students add desert vocabulary to the multilingual word wall (see Figure 3.20). They can find cognates for languages such as Spanish or French.

Figure 3.19   **As We Are Learning: Desert Chart**

Habitat	Image	Animal Life	Plant Life	Vocabulary Related to Habitat
Desert	*Source:* Pixabay.com/falkenpost			

Figure 3.20   **Multilingual Word Wall: Desert**

Desert words English	Desert words Spanish	Desert words Tagalog	Desert words Mandarin	Desert words Arabic	Desert words Korean

Follow-up Activities: A *Walk in the Desert*

Ask students to complete one of the following writing activities. Remind them to use the desert vocabulary they have been learning. Have students self-evaluate their writing using a checklist.

1. You have just spent a day walking in a desert. Write a diary entry telling about what you saw. Get ideas for your entry from *A Walk in the Desert*. Use new vocabulary words you have learned from the story.

2. From the point of view of an animal in the desert, write a diary entry describing your day. Include interactions you have had with other animals and plants. Use new vocabulary words you have learned from the story.

3. Write an adventure story from the point of view of an animal or bird from *A Walk in the Desert*. Include other animals and plants from *A Walk in the Desert* in your story. Use a checklist like Figure 3.21 as a formative assessment that students can complete and the teacher can check.

   • *Lower grades could draw a picture of what they would be most interested in seeing or that they have seen in the desert. In addition, students can share about their pictures with the whole class and the teacher can write down their ideas, as a language experience activity. Then the whole class can read together what they have collectively created.*

Figure 3.21   Self-Assessment Checklist

Name: _____

Did I . . . ?	Yes	No
Use first-person pronouns (I, me, my)		
Write complete sentences		
Begin sentences with a capital letter and end with a period, question mark, or exclamation point		
Use desert vocabulary that I have learned		

From Reading *Roadrunner's Dance*

BEFORE READING: TURN AND TALK

Have students tell about a time they had a problem and someone helped them. Have them connect this experience to *Roadrunner's Dance*.

SAY SOMETHING

Have students read in pairs. Tell them to each read a page and to stop and say something (comment, question, prediction, connection) before reading the next page. Direct students to add new ideas they have learned from the reading to the As We Are Learning chart.

From Reading *Our National Parks*: Post-it Note Activity

- Students get a Post-it note for each page of the reading.
- As they read each page, they write the main idea and a detail on the Post-its (you may want to do the first couple of pages together). Students may write in their home language or in English. Encourage students to use vocabulary directly related to National Parks.
- After reading, students can talk in groups about what they thought were the main ideas for each page (try to come to a consensus if they have different main ideas). Have students discuss new words they are learning.
- Each group shares out with the whole class and the teacher makes a master list of the main ideas with examples of details as well as new vocabulary words the students are learning.

Figure 3.22 Multilingual Word Wall: Parks

Parks words English	Parks words Spanish	Parks words Tagalog	Parks words Mandarin	Parks words Arabic	Parks words Korean

- *Lower-grade students can use Post-it notes to mark and write down key habitat words they see in trade books about habitats. They can add to their multilingual word wall.*

MULTILINGUAL WORD WALL: PARKS

Have students make a master list of vocabulary words about parks to post in the classroom. Then have them add the words for parks to the multilingual word wall (see Figure 3.22).

From *At Home in the Coral Reef*

YOU BE THE TEACHER JIGSAW AND GALLERY WALK

- Students are put in groups of four to five
- Each group is assigned two to three pages of the story
- Each group is responsible for reading their section and making a poster that includes:

  - A drawing (or more than one drawing) to represent their section
  - The main idea and at least one supporting detail from each page
  - New words they have learned about coral reefs
  - Each student in the group initials the sections of the poster they contributed to

- Within their groups, students number off (1, 2, 3, 4 . . .)
- All students with the same number form new groups (ones get together . . .)
- After the posters are placed around the room, the new groups of students do a gallery walk. At each poster, the student who helped make that poster presents their group's work.

- *Lower-grade students can read their grade-level appropriate habitat book and do the jigsaw activity. They can make a drawing of their section, including the important habitat words in their drawing. These students might make drawings of food, water, plants, and other key vocabulary in habitat books.*

AS WE ARE LEARNING CHART: CORAL REEFS

Have students add new information about coral reefs to their As We Are Learning charts (see Figure 3.23).

Figure 3.23   As We Are Learning Chart: Coral Reefs

Habitat	Image	Animal Life	Plant Life	Vocabulary
Desert	*Source:* Pixabay.com/falkenpost			
Coral Reefs	*Source:* Pixabay.com/joakant			

From *Adelina's Whales*

PREREADING: TURN AND TALK

Have students do a turn and talk before reading *Adelina's Whales* using these questions:

- What do you know about whales?
- Have you ever seen a whale?
- What do you know about a whale's habitat?

STORY MAP: STORY BOARD

Have students read the story and fill in Story Map: sequence, character, and setting. (Note: There are a variety of free download story maps to choose from. The version shown in Figure 3.24 is one example.) Read aloud some sections of the story with vivid descriptions, discuss how the writer used description, and then have students write about the setting or one of the characters using descriptive adjectives.

Figure 3.24   **Story Map**

Title		Author	
Setting		Characters	

Beginning	Middle	End

- *Lower-grade students can read a grade-level appropriate book about an animal in an ocean habitat. They can fill in a story map for their story in pairs or as a class.*

After reading *Adelina's Whales,* have students add to their As We Are Learning chart. They can also add to their KWL chart about oceans and to their multilingual word wall.

REVIEW ACTIVITY FOR HABITATS UNIT

Students, working individually or with a partner, pick a favorite habitat and research a famous place related to that habitat (the Painted Desert, the Grand Canyon, Humboldt Redwoods State Park, the Amazon Rainforest, the Great Barrier Reef, the North Sea, or Bora Bora). Create a travel brochure for that place.

To be included in the brochure:

- Pictures
- Description of the place
- Animals you will see
- Plants you will see
- Activities you can do there
- Why this is a great place to visit

To help students as they create their brochures, pass out and review the rubric you will use to evaluate their work (see Figure 3.25). In addition, discuss different persuasive words students can use as they write, such as *must, should,* and *ought to.* Plan to have students share their brochures with other classes or parents at back-to-school night.

Figure 3.25   Travel Brochure Rubric

Name: _____

Does not have pictures	Has one picture	Has two pictures	Has three or more pictures
Has very little description of the place	Has some details to describe the place	Has quite a few details to describe the place	Has many details to describe the place
Does not name an animal found here	Names one animal found here	Names two animals found here	Names three or more animals found here
Does not name a plant found here	Names one plant found here	Names two plants found here	Names three or more plants found here
Does not name an activity that is done here	Names one activity that is done here	Names two activities that are done here	Names three or more activities that are done here
Does not list why this is a great place	Lists one reason this is a great place	Lists two reasons this is a great place	Lists three or more reasons this is a great place

- *Lower-grade students might choose a favorite animal and make a book about that animal and its habitat, including what their animal needs in the habitat.*

BASAL ANCHOR BOOKS FOR THE UNIT

Anaya, R., & Diaz, D. (2000). *Roadrunner's dance.* New York, NY: Disney-Hyperion.

Arnold, C. (1990). *A walk in the desert.* New York, NY: Silver Burdett.

Muir, J. (2017). *Our national parks.* Layton, UT: Gibbs Smith.

Muzik, K., & Brown-Wing, C. (1995). *At home in the coral reef.* Watertown, MA: Charlesbridge.

Sobol, R. (2003). *Adelina's whales.* New York, NY: Dutton Children's Books.

SUPPLEMENTAL READINGS ON HABITATS IN ENGLISH AND SPANISH

Aloian, M., & Kalman, B. (2006a). *The Antarctic habitat.* New York, NY: Crabtree.

Aloian, M., & Kalman, B. (2006b). *The Arctic habitat*. New York, NY: Crabtree.

Aloian, M., & Kalman, B. (2006c). *Water habitats*. New York, NY: Crabtree.

Aloian, M., & Kalman, B. (2007a). *El hábitat de la Antártida*. New York, NY: Crabtree.

Aloian, M., & Kalman, B. (2007b). *El hábitat del Artico*. New York, NY: Crabtree.

Aloian, M., & Kalman, B. (2007c). *Hábitats acuaticos*. New York, NY: Crabtree.

Aloian, M., & Kalman, B. (2007d). *Un hábitat de bosque tropical*. New York, NY: Crabtree.

Aloian, M., & Kalman, B. (2010). *A rainforest habitat*. New York, NY: Crabtree.

Anaya, R., & Diaz, D. (2000). *Roadrunner's dance*. New York, NY: Disney-Hyperion.

Arnold, C. (1990). *A walk in the desert*. New York, NY: Silver Burdett.

Castor, D. (2009a). *Habitats around the world*. Pelham, NY: Benchmark Education.

Castor, D. (2009b). *Hábitats por todo el mundo*. Pelham, NY: Benchmark Education.

Castor, D. (2009c). *What do plants need?* Pelham, NY: Benchmark Education.

Castor, D. (2009d). *¿Qué necesitan las plantas?* Pelham, NY: Benchmark Education.

Cerullo, M. & Rotman, J. (2003). *Sea turtles: Ocean nomads*. New York, NY: Dalton Children's Books.

Cooke, J., & Hsieh, F. (2018). *The sequoia lives on*. Yosemite, CA: Yosemite Conservancy.

Deprisco, D. (2017). *Animals on the move*. Tampa, FL: Scout Books.

Dewey, J. O. (2002). *Antarctic journal: Four months at the bottom of the sea*. New York, NY: Scholastic.

Gibbons, G. (2009). *Coral reefs*. New York, NY: Holiday House.

Greenslade, M. (2016a). *Los osos polares y el hielo del mar Artico*. Temecula, CA: Okapi.

Greenslade, M. (2016b). *Polar bears and the Arctic sea ice*. Temecula, CA: Okapi.

Hamilton, T. (2007). *Animales de Asia*. Pelham, NY: Benchmark Education.

Hamilton, T. (2011). *Animals of Asia*. Pelham, NY: Benchmark Education.

Kalman, B., & Walker, N. (2000). *How do animals adapt?* New York, NY: Crabtree.

Kalman, B. (2006a). *¿Como se adaptan los animales?* New York, NY: Crabtree.

Kalman, B. (2006b). *A forest habitat.* New York, NY: Crabtree.

Kalman, B. (2007). *Un habitat de bosque.* New York, NY: Crabtree.

Kalman, B. (2010a). *Donde viven los animales?* New York, NY: Crabtree.

Kalman, B. (2010b). *My backyard community.* New York, NY: Crabtree.

Kalman, B. (2010c). *Where do animals live?* New York, NY: Crabtree.

Kalman, B. (2011). *Baby animals in ocean habitats.* New York, NY: Crabtree.

Kalman, B, & Crossingham, J. (2006). *Land habitats.* New York, NY: Crabtree.

Kalman, B., & Crossingham, J. (2007). *Habitats terrestres.* New York, NY: Crabtree.

Llewellyn, C. (2012). *Oceans (Habitat Survival).* North Mankato, MN: Capstone.

Lundgren, J. (2011). *Animal habitats.* Vero Beach, FL: Rourke Educational Media.

Macaulay, K. (2007). *Un hábitat de pastizal.* New York, NY: Crabtree.

Macaulay, K., & Kalman, B. (2006a). *A desert habitat.* New York, NY: Crabtree.

Macaulay, K., & Kalman, B. (2006b). *A grassland habitat.* New York, NY: Crabtree.

Macaulay, K., & Kaiman, B. (2006c). *Backyard habitats.* New York, NY: Crabtree.

Macaulay, K., & Kalman, B. (2007a). *Habitats de jardin.* New York, NY: Crabtree.

Macaulay, K., & Kalman, B. (2007b). *Un habitat de desierto.* New York, NY: Crabtree.

McNamara, M. (2009a). *¿Qué necesitan los animales?* Pelham, NY: Benchmark Education.

McNamara, M. (2009b). *What do animals need?* Pelham, NY: Benchmaçrk Education.

Muir, J. (2017). *Our national parks.* Layton, UT: Gibbs Smith.

Muzik, K., & Brown-Wing, C. (1995). *At home in the coral reef.* Watertown, MA: Charlesbridge.

O'Neil, S. (2015a). *Brother elephant.* Temecula, CA: Okapi.

O'Neil, S. (2015b). *Hermano elefante.* Temecula, CA: Okapi.

Sobol, R. (2003). *Adelina's whales.* New York, NY: Dutton Children's Books.

Vieira, L., & Canyon, C. (1996). *The ever-living tree.* New York, NY: Walker.

CHAPTER FOUR

Characteristics of Texts That Support Readers

Our Amazing Oceans Unit

Many basal and alternative language arts programs include a unit of study that focuses on the world's oceans. Some programs expand this unit to include saving our oceans and waters on the Earth. In this chapter, we describe a lower-grade unit of inquiry on oceans, their characteristics, the animals that live in the ocean, and how people can protect and preserve our amazing oceans.

In describing this inquiry unit we discuss both anchor texts from basal reading programs and supplemental texts. When working in classes that include emergent bilinguals, it is important to provide texts that support English learners. In the last chapter, we discussed the importance of providing comprehensible input. In this chapter, we explain the characteristics of texts that support readers by making the reading more comprehensible. Comprehensible written texts help build emergent bilinguals' proficiency in academic English. In addition, we provide a Cultural Relevance rubric that both teachers and students can use to determine if texts are culturally relevant.

CHARACTERISTICS OF TEXTS THAT SUPPORT READERS

When choosing books for emergent bilinguals, teachers should carefully consider whether or not the text has characteristics that support reading (Freeman & Freeman, 2011). Figure 4.1 offers a checklist of the characteristics of texts that support readers. Books with these characteristics help teachers scaffold instruction for students.

Figure 4.1   Characteristics of Text Checklist

☐ Is the language of the text natural? When there are only a few words on a page, do these limited-text books sound like real language, something people really say?

☐ Are the materials authentic? Authentic materials are written to inform or entertain, not to teach a grammar point or a letter-sound correspondence.

☐ Is the text predictable? Books are more predictable when students have background knowledge of the concepts, so teachers should activate or build background.

For emergent readers:

☐ Books are more predictable when they follow certain patterns (repetitive, cumulative) or include certain devices (rhyme, rhythm, alliteration)

For developing readers:

☐ Books are more predictable when students are familiar with text structures (beginning, middle, end), (problem-solution), (main idea, details, examples, etc.).

☐ Books are more predictable when students are familiar with text features (headings, subheadings, maps, labels, graphs, tables, indexes, etc.).

☐ Is there a good text-picture match? A good match provides nonlinguistic visual cues. Is the placement of the pictures predictable?

☐ Are the materials interesting and/or imaginative? Interesting, imaginative texts engage students.

☐ Do the situations and characters in the book represent the experiences and backgrounds of the students in the class? Culturally relevant texts engage students.

The first question on the checklist is, "Is the text natural?" Often books for beginning readers have very limited text, only a few words on each page. Even those books, however, should contain language that sounds natural. By "natural" we refer to language that people use in everyday speech. Natural language helps form a bridge from oral language to written language. Books with natural language are easier to read because the language of the book is more like the language students hear every day both in and out of school.

An example of a book for emergent readers is *Lost in the Fog* (O'Neil, 2019). This book is narrated by a young boy at the beach who gets separated from his father when the fog comes in. It begins, "I was at the beach with my dad and my dog Mac" (2). The language here is similar to everyday speech. The book continues, "Then the fog came in. It hid the trees. It hid the boats. And it hid my dad" (4). The language in the text is similar to the language a young boy would use when telling about the event to a friend.

The second question on the checklist is, "Are the materials authentic?" Authentic books are written to entertain or inform. Many books provide interesting information about the ocean and sea creatures. For example, *Ocean Animals: Who's Who in the Deep Blue* (Rizzo, 2016) has sections on the oceans of the world, the layers of the ocean, coral reefs, and ocean animals and birds. Each page has clear, colorful photographs of the item being described. In addition, the text for each topic is set off in boxes or short sections, and this makes the content more accessible.

Authentic books stand in contrast to some book series in which each book has many examples of a particular phoneme. This was the basis of the early series for teaching a second language, The Miami Linguistic Readers. Books like *The Fat Cat Sat on the Mat* (Karlin, 1996) provide a good example of a book written to provide practice with a particular sound, in this case, the short "*a*" sound. In an effort to use a particular sound or a certain letter pattern, the authors of books like this write texts that do not seem realistic. In this book, for instance, the fat cat sits in a vat or on a mat, and the rat, who is a brat, has a bat.

The third question on the checklist is, "Is the text predictable?" Prediction is a psychological strategy readers use constantly. They predict upcoming words and phrases as well as events or things a character might do. For this reason, many books for beginning readers follow a predictable syntactic pattern. For example, *I'm the Biggest Thing in the Ocean* (Sherry, 2010) contains the pattern "I'm bigger than" on a series of pages. The giant squid states that he is bigger than most of the other sea creatures. The comparative "bigger than" pattern makes the book predictable. Other books have a repetitive pattern or use devices such as rhyme or alliteration, as we point out below when we discuss *Commotion in the Ocean* (Andreae, 2001).

Books are also more predictable when readers have background knowledge about the topic. This is why it is important for teachers to assess and build background knowledge before having students read a text. In the ocean unit described in this chapter, we explain several activities students engage in to build background knowledge about oceans. By organizing language arts curriculum around a big question, teachers build background and make texts more predictable.

The fourth question on the checklist, important for picture books, is, "Is there a good text-picture match?" Pictures provide important nonlinguistic cues for emergent bilinguals. As Rog and Burton (2001–2) point out, one of the factors influencing the difficulty of texts for readers is "the degree of support offered by illustrations" (p. 348). A good example comes from *A Day at the Beach* (Cerini, 2019). Each page begins with "I can see" followed by an object, such as a sandcastle or waves. The consistent syntactic pattern and the photographs of different things found on the beach make the text comprehensible.

For more advanced students, a book with a good text-picture match is *Big Blue Whale* (Davies, 2001). On one of the first pages, an elephant, a giraffe, and two people are superimposed over the picture of a blue whale to give the reader a clear idea of the size of the whale. A later page shows the whale with its mouth open and a clear illustration of its baleen plates hanging down from the roof of its mouth. Although the text is complex, the illustrations make this book very engaging and comprehensible.

The fifth question on the checklist asks, "Are the materials interesting and/or imaginative?" While it is important for books to be predictable, some books, especially books for beginning readers, are so predictable that it is not interesting to read them. Adults won't read a detective story if they can predict the outcome after the first chapter or two. One reason the Agatha Christie novels are so popular is that although the outcomes make sense, they are hard to predict, and the reader becomes very engaged in trying to solve the crime. If books don't engage students, they won't develop a love of reading.

Readers are more engaged when books are interesting and/or imaginative. Guthrie (2004) has conducted research showing that engagement leads to higher levels of reading proficiency. A very interesting and imaginative book about ocean creatures is *Commotion in the Ocean* (Andreae, 2001). This rhyming and rhythmic book begins with an introduction: "There's a curious commotion at the bottom of the ocean" (Andreae, 2001, p. 1). The author then describes crabs, turtles, dolphins, angel fish, jellyfish, sharks, and other sea creatures. Each page has clear illustrations and a description that has rhyme, rhythm, and onomatopoeia. The text describing a lobster, for example, reads, "Never shake hands with a lobster. It isn't a wise thing to do. With a clippety-clap and a snippety-snap he would snip all your fingers in two" (Andreae, 2001, p. 14).

Books can also be engaging when they answer questions students are interested in. Many of the books we list in the ocean unit provide information that students find fascinating. Often, students will choose books on topics they want to know more about. One young student we observed spent hours with a book that gave facts about each baseball World Series. This same student asked for help reading a book about the life of Lou Gehrig, the baseball star who suffered from the disease named after him. Even though this book was difficult for the young student, he was so engaged that he asked for help in reading it repeatedly.

The final question on the checklist asks, "Do the situations and characters in the book represent the experiences and backgrounds of the students in the class?" Books that represent students' experiences and backgrounds are culturally relevant to those students. There has been some confusion about what makes a book culturally relevant. A student who comes to school speaking Spanish may not find a book written in Spanish culturally relevant if the book does not represent the student's own experiences. Many students who enter school speaking Spanish have never been to a Spanish-speaking country. A better approach to determining whether or not a book is culturally relevant is to answer a series of questions about the book. Ebe (2011) and Paulson and Freeman (2003) developed a Cultural Relevance rubric that teachers and students can use to assess the cultural relevance of a book (see Figure 4.2 Cultural Relevance Rubric).

The eight questions on the rubric help teachers and students determine how relevant a particular book is. The first question asks whether the characters are like people the student knows. The second asks whether the student has had experience like those the characters in the story have. The third question deals with the setting, asking if the student has lived in or visited places like those in the story. Students often relate best to stories that are current. Questions five and six ask about the age and gender of the characters. Students generally like to read about characters like themselves.

Question seven gets at the language—not only English, Spanish, or some other language, but also about the language variety the characters speak. A student from South Texas would probably speak a different variety or either English or Spanish than a student from New York. The final question gets at students' experience in reading the genre. Students need repeated opportunities to read each of the different genres, including novels, short stories, plays, and poetry. They need to be given sufficient exposure to each genre so that they can become proficient in reading that genre.

Figure 4.2   Cultural Relevance Rubric

- Are the characters in the story like you and your family?

  Just like us . . . . Not at all

  4   3   2   1

- Have you ever had an experience like one described in this story?

  Yes . . . . No

  4   3   2   1

- Have you lived in or visited places like those in the story?

  Yes . . . . No

  4   3   2   1

- Could this story take place this year?

  Yes . . . . No

  4   3   2   1

- How close do you think the main characters are to you in age?

  Very close . . . . Not close at all

  4   3   2   1

- Are there main characters in the story who are: boys (for boys) or girls (for girls)?

  Yes . . . . No

  4   3   2   1

- Do the characters talk like you and your family do?

  Yes . . . . No

  4   3   2   1

- How often do you read stories like these?

  Often . . . . Never

  4   3   2   1

Teachers we have worked with have used the Cultural Relevance rubric in different ways. As teachers get to know their students, they can use the rubric to match books with readers. Often, teachers rely on a book leveling system, but the factors that determine a book's level cannot determine whether the book is culturally relevant for a particular reader. If students have had experiences like those described in the book, and if they find the text engaging, they will read it even if it is not at their level.

Teachers can also use the rubric during a reading conference with a student who has finished reading a book. Together, the teacher and the student can assess the relevance of the book using the rubric. In addition, teachers can use the rubric with a small group or with a whole class once they have finished reading a text. Finally, some teachers have individual students rate books that they have read by writing answers to each question on the rubric. This provides the teacher with good information as she helps other students choose books.

The checklist applies to books for students at any grade level. However, there are some considerations teachers should take into account if they are teaching older readers whose proficiency level in English reading is well below grade level. Teachers should ask:

1. Is the text limited?
2. Are the pictures, photographs, or other art appropriate for older students?
3. For content texts, are there clear labels, diagrams, graphs, maps, or other visuals?
4. Is the content age appropriate?

English learners in upper elementary may still be at the beginning stages of reading, so it is important that the books they are given do not contain an overwhelming amount of text. Many limited-text books, however, are written for younger students so when looking for books with less text, it is important for teachers to be sure the pictures and other art is age-level appropriate. A sixth-grader may not want to read a book with pictures of baby animals or art showing very young children. Often, books with photographs are more appropriate than books with illustrations.

Many books contain labeled diagrams, graphs, and maps. It is important that the teachers find books with clear examples of these text features and instruct students on how to use this information. For example, the book *Ocean Animals: Who's Who in the Deep Blue* (Rizzo, 2016) uses text boxes on each page under the photograph of the item being discussed. Above all, it is crucial that older beginning readers be given texts that are age appropriate and related to the content they are studying in their other subjects. Many publishers now produce books that have limited text and visual supports with content appropriate for older students.

When teachers use books with characteristics that support readers, they scaffold their reading instruction effectively. Choosing the right books is not easy, and some books are mandated. However, when teachers and students have the freedom to choose their reading, the choices should be based on a good understanding of the characteristics that make texts more accessible. In addition to supporting readers through choosing the right books, teachers can support readers with a number of other strategies, as we show in the units we have described in this book.

PUTTING THE UNIT INTO CONTEXT: FELIPE'S OUR AMAZING OCEANS UNIT

Felipe is a lower-grade teacher in an elementary school in a mid-sized city along the Texas Gulf Coast. Most of the students in his school are the children of immigrants from Mexico and Central America. The school offers a bilingual program, beginning in kindergarten, where students who enter school as dominant Spanish speakers receive instruction in their home language of Spanish and also in English.

Most of Felipe's students can speak and understand conversational English by the time they enter his classroom. He teaches language arts in English and his grade-level partner teaches Spanish language arts. The basal program they use has similar topics and readings in both languages so that students study the same content in both languages. However, Felipe knows he must constantly scaffold his instruction to be sure the English input is comprehensible to his students. He chooses supplemental texts with characteristics that support the readings in the district's required English language arts program. Felipe and his co-teacher understand that teaching around units of inquiry supports their bilingual students. They choose a unit of inquiry on oceans and caring for the ocean, drawing on readings from the basal text. Their big question for the unit is, "What do we find in our amazing oceans, and how do we protect them?"

PREVIEW ACTIVITIES: DRAWING ON AND BUILDING BACKGROUND

Four Corners Activity

Felipe posts several pictures related to the big question about amazing oceans and how we protect them in each of the four corners of the classroom. For example, in one corner he posts pictures of several ocean fish, including whales, sharks, and clownfish. In another corner, he posts pictures of sea turtles and seaweed and baby sea turtles leaving their beach nests and going out to sea. Another corner shows pictures of garbage in the ocean, including an image of the Great Pacific Garbage Patch and another of people throwing their cups and straws on the beach. A final picture is of a coral reef and some animals that live there, including seahorses, jellyfish, sponges, anemones, and seaweed. Figure 4.3 shows the kinds of pictures that could be used for this activity.

Figure 4.3   Four Corners Activity Sample Pictures

| Ocean fish | Sea turtle | Great Pacific Garbage Patch | Trash on the beach |

Sources: Pixabay.com/publicdomainpictures, Pixabay.com/free-photos, Pixabay.com/giogio55, Pixabay.com/adege

Students are put into groups of four and given paper and pencils. Students go to the corner that most interests them and talk about what they see. They write down any words they know related to the pictures in English and Spanish. These become a bilingual list of words they know about the ocean.

- Standards based skills: *draw on background knowledge, make inferences, gather information from pictures, identify known animals and plant life*
- Content objective: *Students will identify sea animals and plants and dangers to them from viewing pictures and discussion.*
- Language objective: *The students will view and discuss pictures and then write vocabulary they know related to the ocean.*

Bilingual Word Wall: Ocean Words I Know

Felipe next asks students to call out some of the words they have on their lists. He knows many of the words are written with invented spelling, so he writes the words on the word wall chart (see Figure 4.4). He asks students to tell him what they talked about and if they know whether the animals or plants need to be protected or not. The class concludes that all the animals and plants in the ocean need protection. They talk about how trash (*basura*) and the plastic they saw in the pictures is polluting the ocean. Felipe and the students then discuss the words *pollution* and *endangered* and determine that much of the ocean is polluted and that life in the ocean is endangered.

Felipe writes the sentence, "Fish are endangered because of the oil spill" on the board. He asks the students, "What is the word that signals 'why'?" The students decide it is *because*. Next he asks if there are other words that tell "why" and one student volunteers *since*. The class discusses how words like *since* and *because* could go at the beginning of the sentence or in the middle, and Felipe writes a second model sentence, "Because of the oil spill, fish are endangered." He explains that the students should use these model sentences and the information on the word wall to write three sentences in their notebooks that tell why some animals and plants are endangered.

Figure 4.4   Ocean Words: Animals and Plants We Need to Protect

English	Spanish	Animal	Plant	Endangered
whale	*la ballena*	x		x
sea turtle	*la tortuga marina*	x		x
coral reef	*el arrecife de coral*	x	x	x

- Standards based skills: *draw on background knowledge, make inferences, students recognize the impact of small things on a whole system; use content-specific academic vocabulary*
- Content objective: *Students will identify life in the ocean and determine that the oceans are polluted and that animals and plants that live in the ocean are endangered.*
- Language objective: *The students will use content-specific academic vocabulary to express what they know about oceans. They will use complex sentences to show cause and effect, following the patterns "<u>Fish</u> are endangered because <u>the ocean is polluted</u>" and "Because <u>of the oil spill</u>, <u>fish</u> are endangered."*

Videos to Build Background: Turn and Talk

Felipe then looks for free videos online that show endangered sea animals and plants. He also finds a video that shows the Great Pacific Garbage Patch and explains how humans pollute the ocean with trash, oil products, and fertilizers. After each video, the students turn and talk in pairs about what they just saw, and each pair writes down words in English or Spanish of animals and plants and things that pollute the ocean. Then the students share the lists they made in pairs and add words to the bilingual word wall. Felipe helps students with animal and plant words they don't know like *kelp* (*quelpo* in Spanish) and *manatee* (*manatí* in Spanish).

- <u>Standards based skills:</u> *draw on background knowledge, make inferences, recognize the impact of small things on a whole system; use content-specific academic vocabulary*
- <u>Content objective:</u> *Students will identify life in the ocean and determine what animals and plants in the ocean are endangered.*
- <u>Language objective:</u> *The students will use content-specific academic vocabulary to express what they know about oceans. They will use the sentence pattern "_____ are endangered because _____ " or "Because _____, _____ are endangered."*

AS WE ENGAGE IN THE UNIT: VIEW ACTIVITIES

Anchor Book and Descriptive Writing

Felipe next asks the students to open their basal text books to the anchor text reading *At Home in the Ocean* (Williams, 2014). Felipe has the students follow along as he reads about whales eating krill, penguins swimming fast in very cold water, turtles laying their eggs in the sand, and sea otters finding food in kelp. The class then adds these animals and plant names to the class bilingual word wall. Felipe calls on his more proficient Spanish speakers to provide the words in Spanish.

At Home in the Ocean includes descriptions of several animals and plants that live in the ocean. For a writing assignment, Felipe asks his students to work in pairs. He asks each pair to choose one ocean animal or plant that they read about in the anchor book and then research additional information about that animal or plant using the ocean unit books he has assembled in the classroom or by conducting an Internet search. When they have gathered information, each pair writes a report on the animal or plant they chose. Felipe explains that they should have at least four specific details to describe the animal or plant. In addition, they should write complete sentences that begin with a capital letter and end with a period. He also reminds them to check their spelling.

Felipe passes out a checklist for students to use to evaluate their writing (see Figure 4.5). He asks them to submit the checklist with their report. He knows that it is important for students to learn to self-assess, and this checklist is a formative assessment that helps the students evaluate their own work.

Figure 4.5 Checklist for Sea Animal or Plant Report

Names: _____

Did We . . . ?	Yes	No
Include four descriptive details		
Include complete sentences		
Make sure all sentences begin with a capital letter and end with a period		
Make sure all my words are spelled correctly		

- Standards based skills: *develop a topic with facts, definitions, and details*
- Content objective: *Write a report with specific details.*
- Language objective: *Describe using specific details. Write complete sentences with proper punctuation.*

Sea Animal Poems: Rhyming Words

Felipe next shows the class the illustrated poetry book mentioned above, *Commotion in the Ocean* (Andreae, 2001). He explains the book describes many ocean animals in a rhyming poem. He asks the students to listen to each poem he reads and tell him what words rhyme. As he reads about crabs, turtles, dolphins, jellyfish, sharks, lobsters, and other ocean life, the students call out the words that rhyme.

As they identify the rhyming words, Felipe writes them on the whiteboard. Different students then go up and circle the sounds that rhyme. Students notice that not all rhyming words are spelled with the same ending letters. For example, while *whale* and *tale* are spelled the same, *size* and *eyes* are not.

- Standards based skills: *recognize and produce rhyming words, recognize that not all rhyming words are spelled the same*
- Content objective: *Students recognize and identify sea animals in a poetry book. Students identify rhyming words.*
- Language objective: *Students will identify the ending sounds of rhyming words in a poem. Students will identify spellings in rhyming words that are the same and different.*

Shape Poetry About Sea Animals

Felipe shows his students a drawing in the shape of a clownfish with words written inside the shape. He asks his students what they notice about the drawing. When they tell him there is writing inside the shape, he explains that students in pairs should look at books in the classroom with pictures of sea animals. They are to choose one sea animal, draw its shape on a paper and compose their own rhyming poem of at least four lines to write inside the shape. He asks them to underline the rhyming words that are spelled the same and put a circle around rhyming words that are spelled differently. Felipe provides an example for them with his clown fish poem (see Figure 4.6).

Felipe passes out a checklist the students can use to evaluate their poems. Figure 4.7 shows the checklist. When students finish writing their poems, they turn in both the poems and the checklist, which Felipe uses as a quick formative assessment for this assignment.

Figure 4.6   Shape Poem

Source: iStock.com/ksenya_savva

Figure 4.7   Checklist for Shape Poem

Name: _____

Did I . . . ?	Yes	No
Choose a sea animal and draw the shape of the animal		
Ensure my poem has at least four lines		
Make pairs of lines rhyme		
Underline the rhyming words that are spelled the same		
Circle the rhyming words that are spelled differently		

- Standards based skills: *recognize and produce rhyming words*
- Content objective: *Students in pairs will identify an ocean animal, draw its shape, and create a short poem about that animal.*
- Language objective: *The students will use rhyming words in a poem to describe their ocean animal. They will recognize that some rhyming words are spelled the same and some are spelled differently.*

Venn Diagram: Oral Report

For the next activity, Felipe wants his students to read more about ocean life and to revisit the text *Commotion in the Ocean* (Andreae, 2001). They reread this text together. Next, he introduces another ocean book, *I'm the Biggest Thing in the Ocean* (Sherry, 2010) by projecting the pages on the whiteboard so everyone can see the words and the pictures. He has his students read the story aloud along with him. As discussed above, in this poem a squid explains he is bigger than many other sea animals, but not bigger than the whale.

When they finish the reading, he asks them to work in groups of three or four to make a list of all the animals mentioned in each book. When they finish, Felipe gives each group a Venn diagram (see Figure 4.8). He explains that they should write the names of animals that are in both books in the overlapping section of the diagram and the names of animals that appear in just one book in the section under the book title. Several animals are the same, including the turtle, jellyfish, octopus, and whale. When the groups finish their Venn diagrams, they post them around the room.

Figure 4.8   Venn Diagram

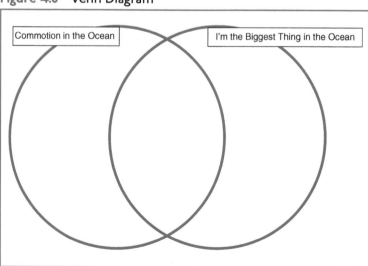

Each group then reports on their Venn diagram by contrasting one sea animal that appears in both books and one that only appears in one of the books. Felipe gives them a sample compound sentence: "The turtle appears in both books, but the shrimp only appears in one book." He writes this sentence on the whiteboard and asks the students to follow this model as they report. He also asks them to listen carefully so that each group can give a different example.

- Standards based skills: *compare and contrast details from stories*
- Content objective: *Students in groups will find details in both stories that are the same and those that are different.*
- Language objective: *Students will report orally on specific details from the stories using a compound sentence.*

"I Am" Poem With Anchor Book: *Down, Down, Down: A Journey to the Bottom of the Sea*

Felipe next shows the class a simple video featuring animals of the ocean, *Ocean Animals,* https://www.youtube.com/watch?v=k COoIZPMAPc. He leads students in a discussion about which of these animals most interests them. Some students like sharks, others choose dolphins, stingrays, seahorses, or whales, and some students are fascinated with sea urchins, octopuses, or sea turtles. Next, Felipe asks the class where in the ocean the animals live: near the surface, deep in the sea, or on the ocean floor? Felipe and the students then read *Down, Down, Down: A Journey to the Bottom of the Sea* (Jenkins, 2009), an informational text that shows different ocean layers and photographs of sea creatures that live in each layer.

Felipe asks students to look online or at books in the classroom library to gather information about a sea animal that interests them. The class brainstorms information they should gather, including color, size, water temperature, habitat, what the animal likes to eat, and whether or not people eat the animal. Next, after brainstorming these ideas, the students and Felipe create an "I am" ocean animal poem together. Felipe provides information on the yellowfin tuna. Together, he and his students write a sample poem about the fish. Felipe also has students help him as he illustrates his poem with a colored picture of a yellowfin tuna (see Figure 4.9).

Felipe points out that his poem begins and ends with the name of his animal following the pattern, "I am a _____." He directs students

Figure 4.9   "I Am" Poem and Fish Drawing

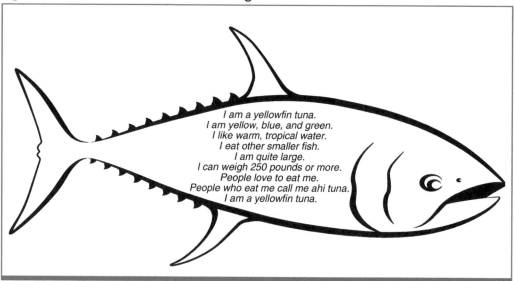

I am a yellowfin tuna.
I am yellow, blue, and green.
I like warm, tropical water.
I eat other smaller fish.
I am quite large.
I can weigh 250 pounds or more.
People love to eat me.
People who eat me call me ahi tuna.
I am a yellowfin tuna.

Source: iStock.com/Marek Trawczynski

to include the information they have gathered about their sea animal in their poem. To help students write their "I am" poems, Felipe hands out a checklist they can use to be sure they include all the required information. He collects the completed checklists and the poems. Figure 4.10 shows the checklist.

Figure 4.10   "I Am" Poem Checklist

Name: _____

Did I . . . ?	Yes	No
Begin and end with an "I am" line		
Include the color of the animal		
Include the size of the animal		
Include the water temperature		
Include the habitat		
Include what the animal likes to eat		
Tell whether or not people eat the animal		

- <u>Standards based skills:</u> *gather information from different sources including electronic sources, write using the information*

- Content objective: *Students will collect information on an ocean animal.*
- Language objective: *The students write an "I am" poem from information they gather using specific details.*

CORAL REEFS: CREATING A FOOD WEB

Felipe wants his students to think about how important oceans, and the animals and plants in them, are to our planet. He begins by introducing coral reefs. He explains a coral reef is an ecosystem that affects the marine life around it.

He gives students a handout listing key words he wants the students to understand and asks them to refer to it as he reads *The Coral Reef* (O'Neil, 2019). He projects the book pages as he reads and asks students to refer to the words on the list (see Figure 4.11). He then shows the class a video on coral reefs, what they are, and the life in them: https://www.youtube.com/watch?v=J2BKd5e15Jc. After reading the story and watching the video, students talk in pairs about what they think the words on the list mean. Each pair writes their own definition for the words.

Figure 4.11 Coral Reef Key Words

Coral Reef: Key Words	What does the word mean?
ecosystem	
marine habitat	
coral polyps	
algae	
zooplankton	
symbiotic relationship	
coral bleaching	

When the pairs finish writing their definitions, the class brainstorms the names of the many types of marine life mentioned in the book and the video (Figure 4.12). Felipe lists these as the students brainstorm. His list includes the following:

Figure 4.12   Felipe's List of Coral Reef Marine Life

- coral polyps
- sea anemones
- algae
- zooplankton
- sea turtles
- parrot fish
- tiger sharks
- clown fish
- cleaner shrimp
- octopuses

One of the key terms on the student handout is "symbiotic relationships." Students work together to make a food web to show how coral, algae, and many fish support each another and how they are all connected. Student pairs are assigned to find information about each kind of marine life on the list and to report back to the class. As students report their findings, they go to the whiteboard and draw arrows showing how different life forms in the coral reef are connected to the marine life they researched. When they are finished, Felipe assigns the student pairs to write an explanation of the symbiotic relationships in the coral reef using a paragraph that has a main idea and supporting details.

- Standards based skills: *use context to confirm understanding, draw on information from multiple print or digital sources, explain relationships or interactions drawing on information they have gathered*
- Content objective: *Students gather information about coral reefs, define key vocabulary, and show connections among the different kinds of marine life in a coral reef.*
- Language objective: *The students orally describe the connections among the various life forms in a coral reef. They work together to write a paragraph with a main idea and supporting details.*

REVIEW ACTIVITIES FOR OCEANS UNIT

Our Oceans in Danger: Persuasive Writing for a Beach Cleanup

As the class studies coral reefs, everything they either read or view in a video mentions how the coral reefs are in danger because of climate change and/or pollution. After the class studies coral reefs, Felipe and his students talk about how our oceans are in danger. Next, Felipe shows them the animated YouTube video story *All the Way to the Ocean* (https://www.youtube.com/watch?v=sZW2ByM623g) and also shows them the book that tells the same story (Harper, 2006). The book and video explain how plastic and other pollutants make their way into the ocean.

Students choose books from their classroom library about how the ocean is changing as a result of changes in climate, plastic and other garbage that has been thrown into the sea, and pollution from emissions like oil spills. They also read about how sea life is dying as a result of both pollution and climate change. Felipe's classroom library includes books in both English and Spanish, and he encourages his students who are more proficient in Spanish to read in Spanish and then report what they learn back in English.

Just as the characters in the video/story *All the Way to the Ocean* did, the students want to help clean up the ocean and stop the pollution. The school where Felipe teaches is located in a town on the Gulf of Mexico. The students ask if they can plan a cleanup field trip to a nearby beach. In order to make the field trip a reality, they decide to take several steps.

1. Plan the cleanup day and list materials they will need.
2. Think about who they can ask to donate gloves and bags to collect the trash.
3. Decide how they can sort the trash for recycling.
4. Find out how they can dispose of other trash.
5. Ask parents to chaperone the trip.
6. Decide the reasons the trip is important and write a persuasive letter to request permission to take the trip.

7. Once they have the details worked out, they will write a persuasive letter to the district superintendent to explain the importance of their planned trip and ask if she will give permission to take this trip and provide a school bus and driver.

As they complete the steps, Felipe works with the class to write their persuasive letter. They begin by brainstorming a list of reasons for making the trip. They list three reasons that they decide are the most important. Felipe guides them as the class works together to write a clear topic sentence that includes the three reasons. Together, they compose the letter with one or two sentences for each reason and a final sentence that summarizes the reasons they have listed. When they finish all the steps on their list, they submit the letter to the superintendent.

Felipe develops a rubric he can use as a formative assessment for this assignment (Figure 4.13). He discusses the rubric with the class and posts it on butcher paper so that the students can refer to it as they write their letter.

Figure 4.13   Rubric for Persuasive Letter

Name	The letter does not include a topic sentence, any specific reasons, or a conclusion	The letter includes a topic sentence but does not have specific reasons or a conclusion	The letter includes a topic sentence, one to two specific reasons, and a conclusion	The letter includes a topic sentence, three or more specific reasons, and a conclusion

Note: The clean-up day could be at the school, in a neighborhood, at a park, or at some other location that has a lot of trash.

- <u>Standards based skills:</u> *write a persuasive letter drawing on evidence they gather related to pollution and global warming; plan and organize a field trip*
- <u>Content objective:</u> *Students gather information about the dangers of pollution, especially plastic, to the ocean. They will also learn about the effects of global warming on the ocean.*

- Language objective: *The students will jointly compose a persuasive letter that includes a topic sentence, specific reasons, and a conclusion that summarizes the reasons.*

Sharing Knowledge: Ocean Mural

Felipe's students have learned a great deal about marine life. They have also learned our oceans are in danger. For a culminating activity, the class decides they want to share what they have learned with the rest of the school by making a large mural of the beach and the ocean to be posted on the wall outside their classroom. They plan to create a mural that includes the sea animals and plants they have studied as well as information about how the ocean is being polluted.

Using large pieces of butcher paper, the class plans out the location of the beach and the ocean on their mural that includes both shallow water, waves, and the deeper ocean. One section will be a coral reef. Different students are assigned different parts of the mural's background and Felipe provides paints and markers.

Once the background is finished, students display it outside the classroom. Next, students make larger versions of the animals and plants they used for their "I am . . ." poems and color them. They place them on the beach (sea turtles, crabs, kelp), in shallow waters and coral reefs (sea otters, sea urchins, starfish) and in the deeper ocean layers (whales, tuna, sharks). Finally, the students bring in plastic bottles, plastic straws, cans, and other trash and attach them to their mural. They also color in an oil spill. On the wall beside their mural, they post a bulleted list of all the dangers to the ocean. They leave blank Post-it notes by their mural and ask students and teachers from other classes to make comments and respond to their mural.

- Standards based skills: *draw on what was learned and demonstrate understanding visually*
- Content objective: *Students demonstrate learning about ocean ecology and the negative effects on the ocean through the construction of a mural.*

YOUR TURN: UNIT REFLECTION

BEFORE TEACHING THE UNIT, REFLECT ON THESE QUESTIONS:

1. Which of the strategies in the unit could you use with your students?

2. How might you modify the strategies for your context?

3. What additional activities might you add?

4. Considering your classroom schedule, how much time will you need to implement the strategies?

AFTER TEACHING THE UNIT, REFLECT ON THESE QUESTIONS:

1. Which of the strategies in the unit did you use?

2. Which activities were most successful with your students?

3. How did you modify the strategies?

4. What additional activities did you add?

5. How much time did you need to implement the strategies?

OUTLINE OF OUR AMAZING OCEANS UNIT STRATEGIES

PREVIEW ACTIVITIES: DRAWING ON AND BUILDING BACKGROUND

Four Corners Activity

Post pictures in each of the four corners of the classroom that relate to the unit's big question, "What do we find in our amazing oceans, and how do we protect them?" For example, one corner could display pictures of several ocean fish, including whales, sharks, and clown fish, and a second corner might have a picture of sea turtles and seaweed next to a picture of sea turtles leaving the beach. A third corner could have pictures of garbage in the ocean, including the Great Pacific Garbage Patch, and people drinking with straws or throwing cups and straws on the beach. The fourth corner could display a picture of a coral reef and the animals that live there. Students go to the corner that most interests them and talk about what they see. They write down any words they know related to the pictures in English and/or Spanish. Their lists become a bilingual list of words they know about the ocean.

Bilingual Word Wall: Ocean Words I Know

Have students share the English and Spanish words on their lists. Write the words on a word wall chart (see Figure 4.14). With the students, decide whether or not the animals and plants on the wall are endangered and need protection and mark that on the chart.

Write this sentence on the board: "Fish are endangered because of the oil spill." Ask the students, "What is the word that signals 'why'?" Point out that *since* can also tell why. Discuss how words like *since* and *because* could go at the beginning of the sentence or in the middle. Write a second model sentence: "Because of the oil spill, fish are endangered." Explain that the students should use these model sentences and the information on the word wall to write three sentences in their notebooks that tell why some animals and plants are endangered.

Figure 4.14   Ocean Words: Animals and Plants We Need to Protect

English	Spanish	Animal	Plant	Endangered?
whale	la ballena	x		x
sea turtle	la tortuga marina	x		x
coral reef	el arrecife de coral	x	x	x

Videos to Build Background: Turn and Talk

Show videos of endangered sea animals and plants and of the Great Pacific Garbage Patch. After each video, have student pairs turn and talk about what they just saw. Direct each pair to write down words in English or Spanish of ocean animals and plants. Also have them write down things that pollute the ocean. Have students share their lists and add words to the bilingual word wall.

AS WE ENGAGE IN THE UNIT: VIEW ACTIVITIES

Anchor Book and Descriptive Writing

Read an anchor text from the basal reader about ocean animals and plants, like *At Home in the Ocean* (Williams, 2014). Have the class add the names of any new sea animals or plants to the bilingual word wall. Next, have the students work in pairs. Each pair chooses one ocean animal or plant that they read about in the anchor book and then researches additional information about that animal or plant. Then have each pair write a report on the animal or plant they chose. They should have at least four specific details to describe the animal or plant. In addition, they should write complete sentences that begin with a capital letter and end with a period, and they should check their spelling.

Provide a checklist for students to use to evaluate their writing (see Figure 4.15). Tell them to submit the checklist with their report. Use this checklist as a formative assessment that helps the students evaluate their own work.

Figure 4.15   Checklist for Sea Animal or Plant Report

Names: _____

Did we . . . ?	Yes	No
Include four descriptive details		
Include complete sentences		
Make sure all sentences begin with a capital letter and end with a period		
Make sure all my words are spelled correctly		

Sea Animal Poems: Rhyming Words

Read aloud the book of sea animal poetry, *Commotion in the Ocean* (Andreae, 2001), and ask the students to listen to each poem and tell which words rhyme. As students identify the rhyming words, write the words on the whiteboard. Have different students then go up and circle the sounds that rhyme. Discuss with the class how not all the rhymes are spelled the same way.

Shape Poetry: Sea Animals

Show the students the clown fish shape poem provided in this book (Figure 4.6) or make up a sea creature shape poem as an example for students. They are to choose one sea animal, draw its shape on a paper, and compose their own rhyming poem to write inside the shape. Figure 4.16 shows a checklist for evaluating the poem.

Figure 4.16 Checklist for Shape Poem

Name: _____

Did I . . . ?	Yes	No
Choose a sea animal and draw the shape of the animal		
Ensure my poem has at least four lines		
Make sure pairs of lines rhyme		
Underline the rhyming words that are spelled the same		
Circle the rhyming words that are spelled differently		

- *Upper-grade teachers may want to use a different text and activity instead of the shape poetry about sea animals. They might do an activity with a text commonly found in basal reading series, Adelina's Whales (Sobol, 2003). First, do a picture walk with the students discussing what they notice in each picture and asking them if they can predict what is happening. Then have the students read the text together in pairs, stopping to mark with Post-it notes anything they do not understand.*

  Next, ask the students to summarize the story by recalling what happens first, second, next, and so forth. Have them discuss what happens each year with the migration of the whales and what the yearly time frame is. Show the students a map of the whale's migration from the Bering Sea to Baja California found on the Internet: http://www.marinebio.net/marinescience/05nekton/GWmigration .htm. Have students work in pairs to write a report on whale migration from Alaska to Baja California and back again, using signal words to indicate sequence.

  Next, divide the students into groups of three or four. Assign each part of the story. They are to look for words that describe and list them in phrases. So, for example, at the beginning of the story students find descriptive words such as the following:

La Laguna is the name of the <u>quiet, dusty</u> village

on the <u>sandy</u> shore

<u>fifty-gallon plastic</u> barrels

a <u>bright, ten-year-old</u> girl

Students report the many adjectives they find, and the teacher writes the list on the board. Then the teacher asks students to write a paragraph using some of the words describing Adelina, the village she lives in, the whales, or the ocean around the village, using as many of the descriptive words they found as possible.

Venn Diagram: Oral Report

Choose two ocean texts, such as *Commotion in the Ocean* (Andreae, 2001) and *I'm the Biggest Thing in the Ocean* (Sherry, 2010). After reading or rereading these texts have students work in groups of three or four to make a list of all the animals mentioned in each book. When they finish, give each group a blank Venn diagram. Explain that they should write the names of animals that are in both books in the overlapping section of the diagram and the names of animals that appear in just one book in the section under the book title. When the groups finish their Venn diagrams, they post them around the room.

Each group then reports on their Venn diagram by reporting on one sea animal that appears in both books and one that only appears in one of the books. Give them a sample compound sentence: "The turtle appears in both books, but the shrimp only appears in one book." Write this sentence on the whiteboard and ask the students to follow this model as they report. Also ask them to listen carefully so that each group can give a different example.

"I Am" Poem With Anchor Book: *Down, Down, Down: A Journey to the Bottom of the Sea*

Show a video about different animals and plants in the sea, such as https://www.youtube.com/watch?v=kC0oIZPMAPc. Read *Down, Down, Down: A Journey to the Bottom of the Sea* (Jenkins, 2009) together and discuss how different animals live at varying ocean depths. Have students choose a favorite sea creature and research it using the Internet, the classroom library, or the school library. Ask students to find information including the color, the size, the temperature of the water it lives in, the habitat, what the animal likes to eat, and whether or not people eat the animal. Next, have students write an "I am" poem using the information. Provide an example like the one in Figure 4.9. Also, have the students draw their animal to illustrate their poem. They may go to the Internet to find ways to draw their animal or plant or look at pictures. Give the students the "I Am" Poem checklist shown in Figure 4.17 to use as they complete the assignment.

Figure 4.17   "I Am" Poem Checklist

Name: _____

Did I . . . ?	Yes	No
Begin and end with an "I am" line		
Include the color of the animal		
Include the size of the animal		
Include the water temperature		
Include the habitat		
Include what the animal likes to eat		
Tell whether or not people eat the animal		

Coral Reefs: Creating a Food Web

Introduce coral reefs as an ecosystem by giving students a key words chart (see Figure 4.18) and reading a book about coral reefs with photos, such as *The Coral Reef* (O'Neil, 2019). The teacher should project the book pages during the reading to help students understand and visualize the key words. Show a video about coral reefs that will reinforce the reading and further help students understand the key words, for example: https://www.youtube.com/watch?v=J2BKd5e15Jc.

Have students brainstorm names of the many types of marine life discussed in the book and video and make a list of them. Figure 4.19 includes coral reef marine life mentioned in the book and video.

Figure 4.18   Coral Reef Key Words

Coral Reef: Key Words	What does the word mean?
ecosystem	
marine habitat	
coral polyps	
algae	
zooplankton	
symbiotic relationship	
coral bleaching	

Figure 4.19   Coral Reef Marine Life

- coral polyps
- sea anemones
- algae
- zooplankton
- sea turtles
- parrot fish
- tiger sharks
- clown fish
- cleaner shrimp
- octopuses

Discuss the symbiotic relationships among the different forms of sea life, then have students create a food web to show how the many plants and animals in the coral reef support one another and how they are all connected. Assign student pairs to research each type of marine life on the list and report back to the class. As students discuss their assignment, they should go to the whiteboard and draw arrows showing how the different life forms in the coral reef are connected. When they are finished, assign the student pairs to write an explanation of the symbiotic relationships in the coral reef using a paragraph that has a main idea and supporting details.

REVIEW ACTIVITIES FOR OCEANS UNIT

Our Oceans in Danger: Persuasive Writing for a Beach Cleanup

Talk with students about how our oceans are in danger. Show the class the animated YouTube video story *All the Way to the Ocean* (https://www.youtube.com/watch?v=sZW2ByM623g), based on the book *All the Way to the Ocean* (Harper, 2006).

Have students further investigate how the ocean is being altered as a result of changes in climate, plastic, and other garbage that has been thrown into the sea, and pollution from emissions like oil spills. Have them read about how sea life is dying as a result of pollution and climate change.

Encourage students to take steps to make their own contribution to the ocean environment through a project. They may take steps such as the following and write a persuasive letter to an appropriate person in charge.

1. Plan the cleanup day and list the materials they will need.
2. Think about who they can ask to donate gloves and bags to collect the trash.
3. Decide how they can sort the trash for recycling.
4. Find out how they can dispose of other trash.
5. Ask parents if they can chaperone the trip.
6. Decide what reasons the trip is important to include in a persuasive letter.
7. Once they have the details worked out, they will write a persuasive letter to the district superintendent to explain the importance of their planned trip and ask if she will give permission to take this trip and provide a school bus and driver. Figure 4.21 shows a rubric for the persuasive letter.

Figure 4.21   **Rubric for Persuasive Letter**

Name	The letter does not include a topic sentence, any specific reasons, or a conclusion	The letter includes a topic sentence but does not have specific reasons or a conclusion	The letter includes a topic sentence, one to two specific reasons, and a conclusion	The letter includes a topic sentence, three or more specific reasons, and a conclusion

Note: The cleanup day could be at the school, in a neighborhood, at a park, or at some other location that has a lot of trash.

Sharing Knowledge: Ocean Mural

A culminating activity to share what the class has learned with the rest of the school could be a large mural of the beach and the ocean. This could be placed on the wall outside the classroom. The mural would include the animals and plants the class has studied and information about how the ocean is being polluted.

Using large pieces of butcher paper, students plan out the location of the beach and the ocean and include both shallow water and waves and the deeper ocean. One section should be a coral reef. Assign students to draw and paint different parts of the background. Once the background is finished and placed outside the classroom, students make larger versions of the animals they used for their "I am . . ." poems and color them. They place drawings of the animals and other marine life on the beach (sea turtles, crabs, kelp), in shallow waters and coral reefs (sea otters, sea urchins, starfish), and in the deeper ocean layers (whales, tuna, sharks). Finally, the students bring in plastic bottles, plastic straws, cans, and other trash and attach them to their drawings. They also color in an oil spill. Finally, next to their mural, students post a statement describing all the dangers to the ocean. They leave blank Post-it notes by their mural and ask people to make comments and respond to their mural. In this way, the class shares what they have learned about the ocean with the whole school, and their peers begin to also think about the importance of preserving our amazing ocean.

BASAL ANCHOR BOOKS FOR THE UNIT

Andreae, G. (2001). *Commotion in the ocean*. Wilton, CT: Tiger Tales.

Jenkins, S. (2009). *Down, down, down: A journey to the bottom of the sea*. Boston, MA: HMH Books for Young Readers.

Sobol, R. (2003). *Adelina's whales*. New York, NY: Dutton Children's Books.

Williams, R. (2014). *At home in the ocean*. Boston, MA: Houghton Mifflin Harcourt.

SUPPLEMENTAL READINGS ON THE OCEAN IN ENGLISH AND SPANISH

Andreae, G. (2001). *Commotion in the ocean*. Wilton, CT: Tiger Tales.

Barnard, B. (2017). *The new ocean: The fate of life in a changing sea*. New York, NY: Knopf Books for Young Readers.

Blackwell, L. (2015). *The life and love of the sea*. New York, NY: Abrams.

Blom, K., & Gabrielsen, G. W. (2019). *Un mar de plásticos*. Lyndhurst, NJ: Lectorum.

Buchanan, S. (2015). *The powerful ocean*. New York, NY: Teacher Created Materials.

Buchanan, S. (2017). *El poderoso océano*. New York, NY: Teacher Created Materials.

Colon de Mejas, L. (2013). *Pesky plastic: An environmental story*. New York, NY: Great Books 4 Kids.

Creasy, M.-A. (2015). *¡Salvemos a las nutrias marinas!* Temecula, CA: Okapi.

Creasy, M.-A. (2019). *Save the sea otters!* Temecula, CA: Okapi.

Davies, N. (2001). *Big blue whale: Read and wonder*. Somerville, MA: Candlewick.

DK Children. (2015). *Ocean: A visual encyclopedia*. New York, NY: DK Children.

Due, J. L. (2017). *Our friends in the ocean: Fun facts about marine animals and sea life*. Scotts Valley, CA: CreateSpace Independent Publishing Platform.

Evans, S. (2017). *National Geographic Readers: At the beach*. Washington, DC: National Geographic Children's Books.

Faust, D. R. (2008). *Sinister sludge: Oil spills and the environment*. New York, NY: Rosen.

Faust, D. R. (2009). *Desastres ecológicos: Los derrames de petróleo y el medioambiente*. New York, NY: Rosen.

Feely, J. (2015a). *La mantarraya que quería volar*. Temecula, CA: Okapi.

Feely, J. (2015b). *La suerte de las nutrias marinas*. Temecula, CA: Okapi.

Feely, J. (2015c). *Mantarrayas*. Temecula, CA: Okapi.

Feely, J. (2016a). *The luck of the sea otters*. Temecula, CA: Okapi.

Feely, J. (2016b). *Manta rays*. Temecula, CA: Okapi.

Feely, J. (2017). *The ray who wanted to fly*. Temecula, CA: Okapi.

Hansen, G. (2017a). *Ballenas*. Chicago, IL: Capstone Classroom.

Hansen, G. (2017b). *Caballitos de mar*. Chicago, IL: Capstone Classroom.

Hansen, G. (2017c). *Delfines*. Chicago, IL: Capstone Classroom.

Hansen, G. (2017d). *Medusas*. Chicago, IL: Capstone Classroom.

Hansen, G. (2017e). *Pulpos*. Chicago, IL: Capstone Classroom.

Harper, J. (2006). *All the way to the ocean*. Claremont, CA: Freedom Three Publishing.

Jenkins, S. (2009). *Down, down, down: A journey to the bottom of the sea*. Boston, MA: HMH Books for Young Readers.

Karlin, N. (1996). *The fat cat sat on the mat*. New York, NY: HarperCollins.

Kenan, T. (2017a). *¡Mira un tiburón!* Minneapolis, MN: Ediciones Lerner.

Kenan, T. (2017b). *¡Mira, un delfín!* Minneapolis, MN: Ediciones Lerner.

Kenan, T. (2017c). *¡Mira, un pez payazo!* Minneapolis, MN: Ediciones Lerner.

Kenan, T. (2017d). *¡Mira, una estrella del mar!* Minneapolis, MN: Ediciones Lerner.

Kenan, T. (2017e). *¡Mira, una medusa!* Minneapolis, MN: Ediciones Lerner.

Kenan, T. (2017f). *¡Mira, una raya!* Minneapolis, MN: Ediciones Lerner.

Lay, P. (2019a). *Deep in the Sea*. Temecula, CA: Okapi.

Lay, P. (2019b). *En lo profundo del mar*. Temecula, CA: Okapi.

Marsh, L. (2010). *National Geographic Readers: Great migrations: Whales*. Washington, DC: National Geographic Children's Books.

Marsh, L. (2012). *National Geographic Readers: Weird sea creatures*. Washington, DC: National Geographic Children's Books.

Marsh, L. (2015). *National Geographic Readers: Grandes migraciones: Las ballenas*. Washington, DC: National Geographic Children's Books.

Musgrave, R. (2016). *National Geographic Kids Mission: Shark rescue: All about sharks and how to save them*. Washington, DC: National Geographic Children's Books.

Muzik, K. (1993). *Dentro del arrecife de coral*. Watertown, MA: Charlesbridge.

National Geographic Kids. (2015). *National Geographic Readers: Ocean animals collection*. Washington, DC: National Geographic Children's Books.

Newman, P., & Crawley, A. (2014). *Plastic ahoy! Investigating the Great Pacific Garbage Patch*. New York, NY: Millbrook.

O'Neil, S. (2016). *Squid*. Temecula, CA: Okapi.

O'Neil, S. (2019). *Awesome oceans*. Temecula, CA: Okapi.

O'Neil, S. (2019). *The coral reef*. Temecula, CA: Okapi.

Palacios, A. (1994). *Sorpresa de Navidad para Chabelita*. Mahwah, NH: Bridgewater Books.

Pallotta, J. (1989). *The ocean alphabet book*. Watertown, MA: Charlesbridge.

Pfiffikus. (2016). *Water, water everywhere! Stop pollution! Save our oceans! Conservation for kids*. Göttingen, Germany: Traudl Wóhlke.

Rattini, K. B. (2015). *National Geographic Readers: Coral reefs*. Washington, DC: National Geographic Children's Books.

Reed, H. (2015). *Las nutrias marinas y el bosque de algas*. Temecula, CA: Okapi.

Reed, H. (2016). *Sea otters and the kelp forest*. Temecula, CA: Okapi.

Reed, H. (2019). *Climate change*. Temecula, CA: Okapi.

Rey, H. A. (2015). *Curious George discovers the ocean*. Boston, MA: HMH Books for Young Readers.

Rice, D. (2011). *Sea life: Time for Kids informational readers*. New York, NY: Teacher Created Materials.

Rice, D. (2012). *La vida marina*. New York, NY: Teacher Created Materials.

Rice, W. (2013). *Animales del mar en peligro*. New York, NY: Teacher Created Materials.

Rissman, R. (2103). *Living and nonliving in the ocean*. Chicago, IL: Capstone Classroom.

Rivas, I. (2015). *Mi mascota*. Temecula, CA: Okapi.

Rivas, I. (2017). *My pet*. Temecula, CA: Okapi.

Rizzo, J. (2010). *Oceans: Dolphins, sharks, penguins, and more!* Washington, DC: National Geographic Children's Books.

Rizzo, J. (2016). *Ocean animals: Who's who in the deep?* Washington, DC: National Geographic Children's Books.

Schreiber, A. (2015). *National Geographic Readers: Los tiburones*. Washington, DC: National Geographic Children's Books.

Seymour, S. (2006). *Sharks*. New York, NY: Harper Collins.

Seymour, S. (2013). *Coral reefs*. New York, NY: Harper Collins.

Seymour, S. (2018). *Sea creatures*. New York, NY: Harper Collins.

Shanahan, K. (2016). *Protejamos los océanos*. Temecula, CA: Okapi.

Shanahan, K. (2017). *El gran concurso de cultivo de calabasas*. Temecula, CA: Okapi.

Shanahan, K. (2019). *Protect the oceans: Act locally*. Temecula, CA: Okapi.

Sherry, K. (2010). *I'm the biggest thing in the ocean*. New York, NY: Dial Books Penguin Random House.

Stewart, M. (2014). *National Geographic Readers: Water*. Washington, DC: National Geographic.

Stewart, M. (2017). *National Geographic Readers: Los delfines*. Washington, DC: National Geographic Children's Books.

Szymanski, J. (2018). *National Geographic Readers: In the ocean*. Washington, DC: National Geographic Children's Books.

Taylor-Butler, C. (2008). *La vida en el arrecife de coral*. New York, NY: Children's Press.

Woolley, M. (2019). *Living with the tides*. Temecula, CA: Okapi.

Young, K. R. (2015). *National Geographic Kids Mission: Sea turtle rescue: All about sea turtles and how to save them*. Washington, DC: National Geograhic Children's Books.

Zommer, Y. (2018). *The big book of the blue*. London: Thames & Hudson.

CHAPTER FIVE

Teaching Academic Language and Meaningful Content

Our Earth, Natural Disasters Unit

In this chapter, we describe an upper-grade unit on the natural disasters that occur all over our Earth. The teacher uses the Equitable Access Approach to make this unit comprehensible and engaging for all the students. We begin the chapter by discussing the reasons for teachers to teach both academic language and meaningful language arts content.

TEACHING ACADEMIC LANGUAGE AND MEANINGFUL CONTENT

As the number of diverse students in schools continues to grow, educators are increasingly aware of how important it is to help emergent bilinguals succeed academically. Mainstream teachers, who once taught primarily native English-speaking children, now find their classrooms filled with children representing different cultures and speaking a variety of languages. While this diversity is enriching, it also presents new challenges. The ESEA (the Elementary Secondary Education Act) points out that it is the legal obligation of states to show that ELs progress in acquiring English proficiency and grade level content knowledge (U.S. Department of Education, 2016, p. 7). In this chapter, we begin by discussing the importance of helping students develop the academic language they need in the content areas. We define academic language and then lay out why it is important to teach language through meaningful content that is sustained in integrated units of inquiry.

As we discussed in Chapter 1, educators can draw on language and content Standards through units of inquiry and connect them to their diverse students' lives and interests. This approach for organizing curriculum is good for all students, but it is especially critical for the academic success of English learners. To help support students in the acquisition of academic English proficiency and academic content, teachers need to connect students to engaging texts and support their understanding of the academic content of those readings.

Academic Language: What Is It?

Academic language is a register of language used in school that is different from the everyday, conversational language we use to communicate in our daily activities. We all use different registers when we communicate in different settings. For example, when Yvonne is talking to her husband about shopping, her children, or her grandchildren, she uses an informal register of language that includes everyday vocabulary and sentence structures that are simple and straightforward. However, when she is talking with her university colleagues about research and theories of second language acquisition, her vocabulary is different from an everyday conversation, and her sentence structures are more complex. Her tone is also different from when she is communicating about family and everyday activities. With colleagues, her tone is authoritative and formal.

Second language learners usually pick up conversational language that allows them to navigate their lives outside of school fairly quickly, in two to three years, but the language of school is not the same as the language they hear on the playground, at the store, or on television shows. For this reason, teachers can often mistake an emergent bilingual who has no accent and seems to be able to carry on a simple conversation as an academically proficient English speaker.

Teachers sometimes believe that students whose home language is not English are not trying in school when they don't do their homework or don't engage in activities in class but appear to speak English well. The real reason is often that those students are not able to read, write, and discuss using the academic register in the texts or understand how to complete academic assignments. These students are able to understand and communicate when the language is context rich and not too cognitively demanding, but once they are presented with complex readings and extended writing assignments, they are lost.

In fact, research has shown that this academic language takes five to seven years for students to acquire (Cummins, 2000). English learners who have been exited from ESL support to mainstream classrooms often lack the academic language proficiency to succeed academically. For these reasons, we are providing supports with strategies to scaffold instruction for the language arts curriculum in the basal reading and supplemental reading programs.

We also provide language objectives with the suggested activities. These language objectives help teachers focus on the academic language they need to teach in order to enable students to read, write, and discuss academic content. Academic language is much more than simply the academic vocabulary that students encounter. While students in language arts, for example, do encounter new vocabulary in the texts they read that may be unfamiliar, students need more than vocabulary alone in order to understand, read, and write academic language.

Language arts students need to learn the academic genres of language arts. These genres include personal recounts, narratives, explanations, and arguments. Each genre has specific components that occur in a predictable order. For example, a personal recount will have a beginning, middle, and conclusion, usually followed by a reflection on what was learned.

In addition, genres are cohesive. Texts are connected through the use of pronouns with clear referents and by nominalization (using the nominal or noun form of a verb). For instance, the student might write, "The main character is **introduced** as an honest person. This **introduction** is later supported in several ways." Here, the sentences are connected by using "introduction," the noun version of the verb "introduce" that occurs in the first sentence. Texts are also connected by signal words showing things like time or cause and effect. In a personal narrative, the signal words show sequence of events, words like *first, next,* and *finally.*

Each genre also has language that is typically associated with the genre. Verbs in personal narratives are generally written in past tense, but words in dialogue are in present tense. In descriptions, writers use adjectives and prepositional phrases to make their language more vivid. By teaching the genres of language arts—including the components of the different genres, ways to connect the parts of the genres, and the language associated with each genre—teachers help students access the curriculum successfully.

Language objectives not only support students but also are a reminder to teachers to consider more than content as they teach. Teachers need to ask themselves in each lesson, "What is the language students need in order to read about, talk about, and write about the content I am teaching?"

Reasons to Teach Language and Content Through Sustained Units of Inquiry

Rather than teaching academic language in isolation through grammar and repetitive exercises, research suggests that academic language is best acquired in the context of meaningful and sustained content. Teaching both academic language and academic content has several benefits. When teachers teach language and content, students learn not only the important academic content that they need but also the academic English associated with the different content areas. As students study content, they are exposed to the language of each academic subject area in a natural context. For example, students learning about natural disasters read interesting books about disasters, interview people who have lived through a natural disaster, watch videos about natural disasters, research natural disasters on the Internet, report to peers, and write about what they are learning. These kinds of activities provide an authentic context for students to develop academic language in a particular area. In addition, since they are learning interesting academic content, students have a real purpose for developing an additional language. Figure 5.1 lists the reasons to teach both language and content.

Figure 5.1   Reasons to Teach Academic Language and Content

1. Students get both language and content.
2. Language is kept in its natural context.
3. Students have reasons to use language for real purposes.
4. Students learn the academic vocabulary of the content area.
5. Students learn the genres of the academic content areas, including the structure of each genre, the cohesive ties that connect parts of the genre, and the language associated with the genres.

We included the word *sustained* in connection with learning language in the context of academic content because it is important to organize the content teaching over an extended period of time (Pally, 2000). For example, it is not enough for teachers to teach the language of disasters by reading one book about a natural disaster, showing some pictures, and doing one activity. When studying a topic like natural disasters, students should read and discuss multiple books on the topic and be involved in a variety of activities. In other words, the content teaching about natural disasters should be sustained over a period of time. Units of inquiry provide multiple opportunities for students to develop academic language as they study content.

PUTTING THE UNIT INTO CONTEXT: GLORIA'S OUR EARTH, NATURAL DISASTERS UNIT

Gloria is an upper elementary school teacher in a large rural school district in California near the San Francisco Bay area. Many of her students have attended school in the same school district since kindergarten. Some students entered school as monolingual English speakers, but many started school as Spanish speakers. The district offers bilingual education for Spanish speakers in the lower grades, but by the time Gloria's students come to her they have usually been exited out of language support programs. Besides native English and Spanish speakers, Gloria has in her classroom students whose home languages include Hmong, Vietnamese, Arabic, Punjabi, and Laotian. All her students speak English, but she suspects that several of her students are long-term English learners (LTELs), that is they speak and understand conversational English but struggle with academic reading and writing. As these LTELs move up the grades, it becomes increasingly critical for teachers to make complex academic content comprehensible for them. Gloria knows this and realizes that when she teaches English language arts using the district-mandated basal program, she must find ways to engage all her students by using activities connected to units of inquiry. The unit of inquiry around the readings in her basal program answer the big question, "What are natural disasters and how do they affect us and the world around us?"

PREVIEW ACTIVITIES: DRAWING ON AND BUILDING BACKGROUND

Using *I Survived* Books

Gloria knows that her students are interested in stories about real people as well as scary stories. She displays several books from Tarshis's *I Survived* book series about how people have survived natural disasters. These books are listed at the end of this chapter. She puts the students into groups of three and asks them to list on a piece of paper at least five different disasters that they identify by looking at the book covers.

She encourages students to read the text on the front and back covers to get more information. Once each group has chosen five disasters, they use their background knowledge and information from reading the covers of the *I Survived* books. Drawing on this information, they compose one sentence describing each disaster on their list. Then, they decide which disaster they think is the most dangerous and tell why.

Gloria asks each group to share their list, the sentence from the disaster they thought was most dangerous, and the conclusion they came to about why that natural disaster was the most dangerous. Lively discussion ensues because students do not all agree on which disasters are the most dangerous. In addition, several of the students share that they or someone they know has experienced one or more of the natural disasters, including earthquakes, hurricanes, forest fires, and tornados. To help her emergent bilinguals as they report, Gloria provides this sentence frame: "_____ are the most dangerous of the natural disasters because _____."

- <u>Standards based skills:</u> *draw on background knowledge, make inferences, gather information from texts*
- <u>Content objective:</u> *Students will identify and describe types of natural disasters from viewing pictures and reading front and back book covers.*
- <u>Language objective:</u> *The students will construct a complete sentence naming a type of natural disaster and give reasons as to why it is the most dangerous using this sentence frame: "_____ are the most dangerous of the natural disasters because _____."*

Natural Disasters KW Chart

Next, Gloria and the students fill out a KW chart, working together (see Figure 5.2). They list the natural disasters they found in the *I Survived* books and for each one they brainstorm what they already know about this type of disaster. They use the sentences they had created in their groups and add questions they now have about each disaster type. For example, for volcanoes, they explain they know very hot rock called lava comes out of the top of a volcano. They want to know how the lava gets hot and how hot it gets. Gloria reminds them that questions that begin with *wh-* or *how* are followed by a verb form. She puts sample questions on the board for students to use as models.

Figure 5.2   KW Chart About Natural Disasters

What do we know about natural disasters?	What do we want to know about natural disasters?
Volcanoes: Hot rock comes out of the top. The hot rock is called lava.	How does lava get hot? How hot does lava get?
Earthquakes	
Hurricanes	
Floods	
Icebergs	
Forest fires	
Tornadoes	

After the students complete this activity, Gloria posts pieces of butcher paper around the room labeled at the top with the names of the different disasters students have talked about. As the unit progresses and students learn more about each disaster type, they will write what they are learning.

- Standards based skills: *draw on background knowledge, make inferences, use content-specific academic vocabulary*
- Content objective: *Students will identify types of natural disasters and explain what they already know about each.*
- Language objective: *The students will use content-specific academic vocabulary to express what they know about natural disasters. They will form* wh- *and* how *questions about natural disasters.*

Building Background: Videos on Natural Disasters

Drawing on the free school resources provided by National Geographic, Gloria then shows the class videos and pictures available on "Extreme Weather on Our Planet" and "Types of Volcanic Eruptions" and "The Oceans and Weather." She also draws on National Geographic's Forces of Nature website for videos and other resources to use with her students.

For each short video, Gloria asks students to discuss with a partner the following questions: "What was the natural disaster that is featured?" "Where did the disaster take place? "What kinds of destruction did the disaster cause?" and "Who was affected by the disaster?" The students then work with their partner to write a one-paragraph summary of the video including the key information they have discussed. Students also add the information to the various disaster charts around the room showing what they are learning.

To help her students write cohesive paragraphs, Gloria explains that a well-written paragraph begins with a topic sentence. She notes that the topic sentence should tell what the natural disaster they viewed was. Then the other sentences should supply details about the disaster. Each of the supporting sentences should begin with a noun phrase or a pronoun that refers to the disaster. She shows them a short model paragraph about a volcano that she has written:

> The natural disaster was a volcano that erupted in Bali. It destroyed the plants and animals living nearby. The volcano also destroyed many houses, and people had to evacuate.

- Standards based skills: *integrate information on a topic from a media source; provide a summary of information*
- Content objective: *Students will identify key information from a video about a natural disaster and its effects on people and the environment.*
- Language objective: *The students will write a cohesive paragraph by starting each sentence with a noun or pronoun that refers to the disaster being described.*

Multilingual Word Wall

Gloria posts a word wall with the different disasters the class is studying listed in the first column (see Figure 5.3). Then she invites students who speak home languages other than English to put an equivalent word from their language in each row. In addition to Spanish, students who speak Hmong, Vietnamese, Arabic, Punjabi, and Laotian add words. Students research on the Internet and ask family members for information. In some cases, students check with parents on how to write the word in their language. To reinforce this content-specific vocabulary, students work in groups to find and print an image for each type of disaster. The groups add their pictures to the chart. When available, students post pictures from their home countries, such as images of floods in Vietnam, hurricanes in India, and the volcano Popocatépetl in Mexico.

Figure 5.3 Multilingual Word Wall for Natural Disasters

English	Image	Spanish	Hmong	Arabic	Vietnamese	Punjabi	Laotian
Earthquake	*Source:* Pixabay.com/Angelo_Giordano						
Forest fire	*Source:* Pixabay.com/Ylvers						
Flood	*Source:* Pixabay.com/jsptoa						
Hurricane	*Source:* Pixabay.com/12019						

(Continued)

(Continued)

Tornado	*Source:* Pixabay.com/lurens		
Iceberg collision	*Source:* Pixabay.com/comfreak		
Volcano	*Source:* Pixabay.com/julius_silver		

I Survived Book Posters

Gloria forms groups of three to four students. Some groups are made up of students who speak the same home language. She gives each group an *I Survived* book to read together and then make a poster listing the theme of each book, summarizing the key events and details of the disaster, and explaining how the main characters survived the disaster featured in the book. Figure 5.4 shows the directions for this assignment.

Once the groups finish their posters, they display them around the room, and each group makes a presentation about the book they read. The posters are left up for reference throughout the unit.

- <u>Standards based skills:</u> *determine main ideas or themes in a text, provide supporting details, list key events*
- <u>Content objective:</u> *Students will identify the characteristics of a natural disaster and its effects on people and nature.*
- <u>Language objective:</u> *In their oral presentation, students will list key events in order of occurrence using sequence signal words. Students will use descriptive adjectives as they describe how the characters survived.*

Figure 5.4 Directions for the *I Survived* Poster Assignment

Read the *I Survived* book as a group	Write the title of the *I Survived* book on your poster	Illustrate the disaster or find a picture on the Internet
List in order the main events.	For each event, include descriptive details.	Illustrate key events or find pictures on the Internet.
Describe the main character.	Give details about the main character.	Choose descriptive words to describe how the main character felt.
How did the character survive?	Supply details of how he/she/they survived.	Draw or find pictures to show how the character survived.

AS WE ENGAGE IN THE UNIT: VIEW ACTIVITIES

Finding Textual Evidence

The first anchor text for the basal program Gloria uses focuses on one natural disaster, volcanoes. The first piece students read from their language arts program, *Volcanoes* (Seymour, 2006), is written by well-known science author Simon Seymour, who writes for children and young adults. In his beautifully illustrated text, Seymour illustrates and describes volcanoes beginning with the beliefs early people had about volcanoes and then describing types of volcanoes and showing how they are formed. He discusses different volcanoes, including Mount St. Helens and its eruption.

Gloria first has the students turn the pages of their books as she projects each page on the whiteboard. She asks students to comment on the photographs and on anything they notice during a quick picture walk through the text. Then, she directs students to read through the text on their own. She asks students to pick out the main idea from each section and then list one or two sentences from the text that provide textual evidence to support that main idea. For example, at the beginning of the book, a main idea is that ancient people had different beliefs about what caused volcanoes. Students list the idea and the textual evidence to support their choice. Gloria works with the students to write the first two entries for the main idea and textual evidence chart shown in Figure 5.5.

Figure 5.5   Main Idea and Textual Evidence Chart

Main idea	Textual evidence	Textual evidence
Ex #1: Ancient groups had different beliefs about volcanoes.	**Ex #1:** Early Romans believed Vulcan, their god of fire, worked at a hot forge to make weapons.	**Ex #1:** Vulcan's forge made sparks.
Ex #2: Our planet is made up of many layers of rock.	**Ex #2:** The top layers are the crust.	**Ex #2:** Deep beneath the crust is hot, molten magma.

Since many of her students have not developed grade-level reading and writing skills, Gloria decides to conduct a formative assessment of the students' writing. She uses a rubric for this assessment. Figure 5.6 shows the rubric she used.

Figure 5.6   Rubric for Writing Assignment

Only one or two complete sentences	Some complete sentences	Most of the sentences are complete	All of the sentences are complete
None or few of the sentences start with a capital letter and end with a period.	Some of the sentences start with a capital letter and end with a period.	Most of the sentences start with a capital letter and end with a period.	All the sentences start with a capital letter and end with a period.
Student identifies few of the main ideas.	Student identifies some of the main ideas.	Student identifies most of the main ideas.	Student identifies all the main ideas.
Student chooses textual evidence that fits only a few of the main ideas.	Student chooses textual evidence that fits some of the main ideas.	Student chooses textual evidence that fits most of the main ideas.	Student chooses textual evidence that fits all of the main ideas.

- Standards based skills: *determine main ideas or themes in a text and provide textural evidence, provide supporting details, list key events*
- Content objective: *Students will identify types of volcanoes, how they are formed, and how and why they erupt.*
- Language objective: *Drawing on the information in the text, students will write complete sentences to indicate key ideas and supporting textual evidence.*

Found Poems

The next day, students meet in groups and share their main ideas and the textual evidence they found to support each idea. In order to further help students understand their reading and learn the academic vocabulary included in it, Gloria asks each group to write a found poem. She gives students strips of paper and has them choose phrases and key words from their main ideas and textual evidence charts and write those words and phrases on their slips of paper. Then she asks students to put the words and phrases in an order that makes sense to them to create a found poem that represents what they now know about volcanoes. She explains that they can repeat key words or phrases to make their poems if they wish.

Students move their slips of paper around until they like the sound of their poems. Gloria then gives each group a piece of butcher paper and directs them to write their poem on the paper and illustrate it. The groups post their found poems around the room. Once all the groups have posted their poems, Gloria asks each group to present their poem to the class. The students meet in groups to decide how to perform their poem. Some groups read their lines in unison, and some groups have each member read a few lines. Some groups read sections of their poem in pairs. By the time all the groups have presented their found poems, all the students in the class have had a thorough review of the key ideas and textual evidence from their reading about volcanoes.

- Standards based skills: *determine main ideas or themes in a text, provide supporting details, list key events, create a poem, and illustrate key ideas*
- Content objective: *Students will identify the key concepts related to volcanoes and give textual evidence to support them through a found poem*
- Language objective: *Students will identify key words or phrases from a text and combine these into a found poem.*

Historical Fiction: *The Dog of Pompeii*: Fact or Fiction?

A second anchor text about volcanoes from the basal reader is the short story *The Dog of Pompeii*, a piece of historical fiction (Untermeyer, 1932). This is the tale of a blind boy and his dog living in the ancient Roman city of Pompeii in AD 79 at the time of the eruption of Mount Vesuvius. The story captures the imagination of all Gloria's students, especially after they view a video showing the preserved stone remains of the city after the volcanic eruption that occurred over 2,000 years ago. Among those stone remains is a dog with a piece of bread in its mouth. Untermeyer takes the historical account and the ossified remains of the dog to create this story that has fascinated readers across time.

Gloria explains that *The Dog of Pompeii* is historical fiction, a literary genre that is set in a particular historical context and preserves the customs and social conditions of the period. At the same time, the characters and events are creations of the author's imagination. This literary genre combines fact and fiction to make history come alive for readers. As a first step in understanding this genre, Gloria has the students fill in a chart with complete sentences listing at least five details about the characters or events in the story. She asks them to decide if each detail is fact or fiction and explain why they thought it was fact or fiction. To help them write sentences to explain why they decided the detail is fact or fiction, Gloria writes a model sentence on the board: "The blind boy in the story is fiction because no one knows the people who lived in 79 BC." She reminds the students that their "why" sentence should include a signal word like *because* to show cause and effect. Figure 5.7 shows an example chart.

Figure 5.7   Fact or Fiction Chart

Detail about character or event	Fact? Or fiction?	Why?

- <u>Standards based skills:</u> *identify details from a historical fiction text, determine if fact or fiction, support conclusions*
- <u>Content objective:</u> *Students will identify details from* The Dog of Pompeii *and determine if the details are historical facts or fiction created by the author.*

- <u>Language objective:</u> *Students will write complete sentences using signal words like because showing cause and effect to support their conclusions.*

Writing and Performing a Myth

Seymour's book, *Volcanoes* (2006), begins with two beliefs ancient peoples had about volcanoes. Gloria decides to ask her students to conduct research using Internet sources to find other myths and legends about natural disasters. Students work in pairs and find different myths. Several students with roots in other countries search for myths from that country. Each pair chooses a myth and writes down the details to share with the rest of the class.

Next, Gloria tells the class that they will write a short play based on the myth they have researched about a natural disaster. She explains that the play should answer questions such as: What might have caused it? Who might have caused it? What were the results? Students brainstorm ideas and then each pair writes a short play to illustrate their myth.

To prepare the students for writing their plays, Gloria projects the cover and the first few pages of one of the plays in the book *10 Minute Plays for Kids of All Ages* (Griffith, 2016). She asks the students to talk in small groups and make a list of what they notice about the differences between the way the myths they have researched are written and a play is written.

The students report back. Gloria leads a class discussion about the differences between the way myths and plays are written. The class brainstorms several differences. Myths are written using the past tense, but plays are written in the present tense. Myths may include dialogue that is written in present tense and marked by quotation marks. Plays also contain dialogue, but there are no quotation marks. Myths are written in paragraphs, but in writing a play, writers put down the character's name and a colon or dash and then write what the character says, but there are no quotation marks. Plays also might have stage directions telling what the character does. At the beginning of a play, there might be a short description of the setting. Gloria writes these ideas on the whiteboard. Students add more differences as they read myths and write their plays. This helps them to understand the differences between these two genres.

The students enjoy writing their plays, sometimes referring to Greek mythological characters they studied in the past, sometimes using superheroes, sometimes referring to myths they read about from their home countries, and sometimes creating new mythical creatures.

When they perform their plays the following day, many bring costumes and props from home.

- Standards based skills: *work collaboratively with others to create a narrative; write a drama from the narrative and perform it*
- Content objective: *Students write a myth about the reasons for a natural disaster and convert it to a drama to perform.*
- Language objective: *Students recognize the difference between two genres, a myth and a play. They write a play using the conventions of the genre.*

Exploring the San Francisco Earthquake of 1906

On the Smart Board, Gloria shows students pictures from the Internet of the San Francisco earthquake of 1906. Gloria then plays a video that shows how earthquakes occur. Students talk about earthquakes. Many of them have experienced an earthquake, since their town is near the San Andreas fault. They also note from the video that volcanoes can cause earthquakes.

Next, Gloria reads *Quake! Disaster in San Francisco, 1906* (Karwoski, 2006) a trade book about the San Francisco earthquake of 1906. Students listen to the story as the teacher reads it, and they write the answers to the following questions:

1. Why did so many people come to live in San Francisco in the first place?
2. What causes earthquakes?
3. Did the people of San Francisco get any warnings before the big earthquake hit? What were they?
4. Why were so many buildings destroyed in that earthquake?
5. What are people doing today to be safer in the case of an earthquake?

After the reading, students share their answers in pairs. Gloria leads a class discussion as students report back. Because most of the students have experienced some small earthquakes, much of the discussion centers around the possibility of another big earthquake occurring nearby soon.

- Standards based skills: *integrate information from visual, media, and oral sources and evaluate what they hear*

- Content objective: *Students will identify key ideas about earthquakes from visuals, media, and an oral text.*
- Language objective: *Students will identify specific information as they listen to an oral reading and share their answers orally answering "why" questions with reasons and "what" questions with descriptive words and phrases.*

If I Lived on an Iceberg/Glacier

The next anchor text in the basal reading unit is another book by Simon Seymour, *Icebergs and Glaciers* (2018). Before reading the text, the students look with Gloria at pictures of both icebergs and glaciers. Since they live in California and few have had much experience with any kind of real cold, ice, or snow except for a trip to the mountains, Gloria asks the students to write answers to the following questions based on the pictures from the text. These questions ask students to rely on different senses and use conditional sentences.

- If I lived on a glacier, what would I see?
- If I lived on a glacier, what would I hear?
- If I lived on a glacier what activities would I do?

Gloria then reads the story aloud, and the students follow along in their language arts textbooks. Gloria also calls on individual students to read some of the sections. Once they finish the reading, Gloria has the students go back to the questions and add more details, drawing on the reading.

- Standards based skills: *form and use sentences with conditional mood, draw information from a text they read and make conclusions*
- Content objective: *Students will predict what one sees, hears, and does in a glacial climate.*
- Language objective: *Students will write conditional sentences using the frame "If _____, I would _____."*

Sequence Chart and Paragraph Writing Activity From Anchor Text *Icebergs and Glaciers*

Next, students are given a sequence chart (Figure 5.8) and asked to explain the steps, in order, of how a snowflake eventually can become an iceberg or a glacier, using information from their anchor text, *Icebergs and Glaciers,* and the Internet. They draw each stage

Figure 5.8   Sequence Chart

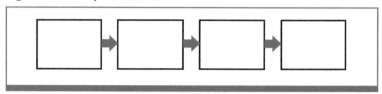

and then write in the text boxes what happens during each step. Students complete the graphic individually and then share their answers with a partner, making changes as needed if they realize they did not complete their sequence chart correctly. Then, working individually, students write a paragraph to explain the steps in the formation of an iceberg or a glacier. They use signal words showing sequence to connect the sentences in their paragraph.

To help her students write good paragraphs, Gloria gives them a checklist they can use to evaluate their finished paragraphs (see Figure 5.9). The students complete the checklist and turn it in with their paragraphs. Then Gloria uses the students' checklists to see how well they understand how to write a good paragraph.

Figure 5.9   Checklist for Process Paragraph

Name: _____

Did I . . . ?	Yes	No
Indent the first line of the paragraph		
Begin with a topic sentence that introduces the steps		
Write complete sentences		
Connect the sentences with signal words showing sequence		
Write a concluding sentence that sums up the steps in the process		

- Standards based skills: *determine the sequence of a process, explain the steps in the process*
- Content objective: *Students will identify the sequence of steps in the process of a snowflake becoming a glacier or an iceberg.*
- Language objective: *Students will write a paragraph using signal words to show a sequence of events.*

KWL: The *Titanic*

Gloria next asks her class what they know about the *Titanic*. Many students have seen the movie about the sinking of the *Titanic*, and a few had even read about it before. Students know that an iceberg was responsible for the ship's sinking and that the ship was supposed to be unsinkable. Gloria decides to have the class do a KWL chart about the *Titanic* (see Figure 5.10) before they begin to read their anchor text, *Exploring the* Titanic (Ballard, 1988). Since the text has many details about the *Titanic* and the sinking, she knows that they will learn a lot about the *Titanic* to add to the KWL chart.

Figure 5.10   KWL Chart: The *Titanic*

What do we know about the Titanic?	What do we want to know about the Titanic?	What have we learned about the Titanic?

Identifying Narrative and Facts in Narrative Nonfiction

Gloria explains to students that their reading, *Exploring the* Titanic, is narrative nonfiction. In narrative nonfiction, the author uses elements of fiction, including plot, setting, conflict, and character development, but bases the narrative on facts from original source materials such as photographs, reliable accounts, and quotes from real people. Narrative nonfiction is similar to historical fiction because it is based on facts but written in fictional form. In both cases the author begins with actual events but uses a fictional style to tell about the event. The class talks about the author, Robert Ballard, who actually found the wreck of the *Titanic* on the ocean floor and discovered many details about the shipwreck.

Gloria has students fill out two graphics for this reading. First, she asks students to identify narrative elements including plot, setting, and conflict. She also has students name four characters and tell about them and why they were on the *Titanic*. She asks them to describe each character, giving basic details. This chart is shown in Figure 5.11.

The second graphic (Figure 5.12) is a chart similar to the one the students completed after reading *The Dog of Pompeii*. She asks students

Figure 5.11   Narrative Events: The *Titanic*

Narrative		
Plot:	Setting:	Conflict:
Characters		
Character 1:	Character 2:	Character 3:	Character 4:

Figure 5.12   Fact or Fiction Chart: The *Titanic*

Detail about character or event	Fact? Or Fiction?	Why?

to choose five details about characters or events to decide if each detail is fact or fiction, and then explain why they thought it was fact or fiction.

After completing their graphics, students share their answers with a partner and explain each of their decisions. Then, Gloria leads the class in creating a master chart for the text, listing details of characters and events, labeling them as fact or fiction, and giving reasons for their decisions.

- Standards based skills: *identify elements of narrative writing including plot, setting, and character; use textual evidence and make inferences to identify facts within a narrative nonfiction*
- Content objective: *Students will read a narrative nonfiction and identify important details of the sinking of the* Titanic.
- Language objective: *Students will provide explanations orally using complex sentences showing the reasons that the details are fiction or nonfiction using the sentence frame "Since _____, I decided _____."*

REVIEW ACTIVITIES FOR NATURAL DISASTERS UNIT

Writing Narrative Nonfiction (Historical Recount) About a Natural Disaster

Gloria then asks her students to get back into the same groups they were in for their *I Survived* book posters. She points out to the students that they have just read and analyzed the narrative nonfiction *Exploring the Titanic* from their basal reading program and that they have also read a similar genre, the historical fiction *The Dog of Pompeii*. In addition, they read the *I Survived* books. She explains that historical nonfiction contains elements of the genre historical recount. Historical recounts include an orientation to the historical event, the sequence of the event, and a conclusion. All these fictional stories have a factual base, and the texts include a combination of a narrative including character, settings, and plot and elements of an historical recount drawn from real events.

Next, Gloria has the groups choose a natural disaster from either their *I Survived* book and poster or another natural disaster they are interested in. They research source material for the natural disaster they choose. They brainstorm their own narrative nonfiction, inventing characters and a plot. Students then coauthor and illustrate a short narrative nonfiction story around a natural disaster that occurred. The students are directed to include events from the sources they find and to also include a narrative story about a character or characters dealing with the disaster.

Figure 5.13   Rating Scale for Narrative Nonfiction

Name: _____

How well did the student . . . ?	Needs Work	Fair	Good	Excellent
Explain the plot				
Describe the setting				
Describe the characters				
Include an orientation				
Put the events in sequence				
Include a conclusion				

Gloria creates a rating scale for a formative assessment of this assignment. This allows her to determine how well the students include the required elements of a narrative nonfiction story. Figure 5.13 shows the rating scale she uses.

- <u>Standards based skills:</u> *produce elements of narrative writing including plot, setting, and character working collaboratively; using textual evidence from informational reading including original sources, include facts based on sources to create a narrative nonfiction using the genre historical recount*
- <u>Content objective:</u> *Students will create a narrative nonfiction about a natural disaster that has occurred and include important details of the event.*
- <u>Language objectives:</u> *Students will collaborate to write their own nonfiction narrative including facts from sources with elements of an historical recount including an orientation, sequence of events, and conclusion. In addition, the text will include fictional elements of a narrative including plot, setting, and characters.*

Sierra: A Poem Demonstrating Personification

The final anchor reading for the basal unit on nature and natural disasters is the illustrated poem *Sierra* (Siebert, 1996). Gloria reminds the students about figurative language they have studied in lower grades. She points out that in the poem *Sierra* the author uses personification, a type of figurative language that gives human qualities to nonhuman things. In the poem, a mountain in the Sierra mountain range is speaking as if it were a person.

Since the class has been studying forces of nature, Gloria asks the students to listen as she reads the poem and notice places in the poem where the mountain talks about how the forces of nature have affected her. As she reads, the students underline the parts of the poem where forces of nature have been affecting and changing the mountain. The class discusses how earthquakes and maybe volcanoes formed the mountain and how strong winds wear her down. They also notice how the poet uses personification, since the mountain speaks like a person and refers to other mountains as her sisters that stand like sentinels.

After reading the poem and identifying the examples of personification, Gloria asks students to choose a partner to write their own poems using personification. They are to choose a geographical feature (like the ocean, a river, a volcano, a rain forest, a lake) or a natural disaster (like an earthquake, a tornado, a blizzard, a drought, or a tsunami) and write a poem using personification. They create an illustrated poster with their poems. Once they complete their poems, the partners read them to the class in two voices with each student reading different stanzas. The poem posters and the *I Survived* book posters are then displayed on the bulletin board outside the classroom to show the whole school how the students have been reading, writing, and discussing natural disasters.

- Standards based skills: *interpret figurative language such as personification; produce a poem with personification; read poetry aloud with accuracy and expression*
- Content objective: *Students will identify forces of nature that affect the mountain and write and illustrate a poem using personification related to nature or a natural disaster.*
- Language objectives: *Students will write their own poems about natural occurrences in nature using personification and precise, descriptive language.*

YOUR TURN: UNIT REFLECTION

BEFORE TEACHING THE UNIT, REFLECT ON THESE QUESTIONS:

1. Which of the strategies in the unit could you use with your students?

2. How might you modify the strategies for your context?

3. What additional activities might you add?

4. Considering your classroom schedule, how much time will you need to implement the strategies?

AFTER TEACHING THE UNIT, REFLECT ON THESE QUESTIONS:

1. Which of the strategies in the unit did you use?

2. Which activities were most successful with your students?

3. How did you modify the strategies?

4. What additional activities did you add?

5. How much time did you need to implement the strategies?

CONCLUSION

Teachers are expected to help all their students, including their English learners, meet Standards using a language arts curriculum designed for native English speakers. The units we have described in this book show how teachers in mainstream classes can make mandated language arts curriculum accessible to all their students by using the Equitable Access Approach. Improving instruction for English learners is no easy task. Some students may have suffered from trauma. ELs are expected to learn academic English in a very short time. In addition, they may lack background knowledge in one or more content areas. Effective language arts instruction based on the Equitable Access Approach can help emergent bilinguals become more engaged in the process of developing the reading and writing proficiency they need to meet the challenges they face.

Our goal has been to describe in detail units of study consistent with the approach. The teachers all follow key practices for teaching emergent bilinguals. They organize their instruction around units of inquiry; include activities that enable them to learn about their students; create a multilingual, multicultural environment; assess students' language proficiency; use a gradual release of responsibility model for reading and writing; draw on students' backgrounds and cultures; and draw on students' home languages by using translanguaging strategies. These teachers write language and content objectives. They use strategies to make the academic input comprehensible. They consider characteristics of the texts they use. And they teach both language and content to build academic language.

When teachers adopt the Equitable Access Approach, their emergent bilinguals can succeed. English learners find the language arts curriculum meaningful and engaging. They draw on all their language resources and enrich classroom discussions and activities. As a result, they develop both academic English and content knowledge. The Equitable Access Approach is not simply an add-on for English learners. Rather it is a way of teaching that can help all students meet the challenge of the Standards.

It is our hope that, as you have reflected on and implemented the strategies we describe in each chapter, you have seen greater involvement of your students in your rigorous language arts curriculum and improvement in their English academic proficiency. We hope you will continue to use the Equitable Access Approach as you implement these strategies and similar ones in other units in your language arts curriculum.

OUTLINE OF NATURAL DISASTERS UNIT STRATEGIES

PREVIEW ACTIVITIES: DRAWING ON AND BUILDING BACKGROUND

Drawing on Background Knowledge Using *I Survived* Book

Have students look at pictures or book covers showing natural disasters and then, working in small groups, list five disasters they can identify. Through discussion and information they gather from the books or the Internet, have them decide which disaster is the most dangerous and why. Direct them to write a complex sentence showing cause and effect using the sentence frame "_____ are the most dangerous of the natural disasters because _____."

- *Lower-grade students can read or listen to books about natural disasters that are accessible to their grade levels. They identify the disaster and the causes of the disaster. If the reading is fictional and based on a natural disaster, the students discuss how the natural disaster affected the characters in the story.*

Natural Disasters KW Chart

Have students work in groups to list what they know about natural disasters and what they want to know. As they report back, fill in

Figure 5.14   KW Chart About Natural Disasters

What do we know about natural disasters?	What do we want to know about natural disasters?
Volcanoes: Hot rock comes out of the top. The hot rock is called lava.	How does lava get hot? How hot does lava get?
earthquakes	
hurricanes	
floods	
icebergs	
forest fires	

a KW chart with information about the different natural disasters (see Figure 5.14). Remind students that questions that begin with *wh-* or *how* are followed by a verb form and write sample questions on the board for students to use as models. As the unit continues, students add new questions and what they have learned.

Building Background: Videos on Natural Disasters

Use free school resources from sites on the Internet, including *National Geographic*. Have students watch these videos about natural disasters that have occurred and then discuss with a partner the following questions:

- What was the natural disaster featured in the video?
- Where did the disaster take place?
- What kinds of destruction did the disaster cause?
- Who was affected by the disaster?

The students then write a paragraph summary of each video including the key information they discussed. To help students write cohesive paragraphs, explain that a well-written paragraph begins with a topic sentence and that the other sentences should supply details about the disaster. Each of the supporting sentences should begin with a noun phrase or a pronoun that refers to the disaster. Show students a short model paragraph.

- *Lower-grade students can discuss videos about natural disasters appropriate for younger students and, in small groups, write a sentence about what they learned about each disaster.*

Multilingual Word Wall: Natural Disasters

Using the list of natural disasters that the class posted for the KW chart, post another chart and have students do an investigation of the words for each natural disaster in the home languages of the students in your class. Also post a picture from the Internet or other sources of each. If there are available pictures from the students' home countries, such as the Popocatépetl volcano in Mexico, then use those photographs (see Figure 5.3).

I Survived Book Posters

Organize students into groups of three or four. Some groups may be organized by the same home language. Give each group an

I Survived book to read together and then have them make a poster listing each book's theme, summarizing the key events and details of the disaster, and explaining how the main characters survived the disaster featured in the book. They should add illustrations to their posters. To help them, post directions for the assignment (see Figure 5.15). Have students present their posters, which are displayed around the room.

Figure 5.15   Directions for the *I Survived* Poster

Read the *I Survived* book as a group	Write the title of the *I Survived* book on your poster	Illustrate the disaster or find a picture on the Internet
List in order the main events.	For each event include descriptive details.	Illustrate key events or find pictures on the Internet.
Describe the main character.	Give details about the main character.	Choose descriptive words to describe how the main character felt.
How did the character survive?	Supply details of how he/she/they survived.	Draw or find pictures to show how the character survived.

- *Lower-grade students can choose a natural disaster and read about it in grade appropriate books or on the Internet. They can make posters about the disaster including where and when it happened, what destruction it caused, and how it affected the people involved in it. They also can illustrate their posters.*

AS WE ENGAGE IN THE UNIT: VIEW ACTIVITIES

Finding Textual Evidence

Do a picture walk through the basal anchor text, *Volcanoes* (Seymour, 2006). Next have students read the text and fill out the textual evidence chart, picking out main ideas and supplying textual evidence for each main idea in each section of the reading. Remind students to use complete sentences as they fill in their charts (see Figure 5.16). Work through one or two examples to model the process. Use the rubric (Figure 5.17) to evaluate this assignment.

Figure 5.16   Main Idea and Textual Evidence Chart

Main idea	Textual evidence	Textual evidence
Ex #1: Ancient groups had different beliefs about volcanoes.	**Ex #1:** Early Romans believed Vulcan, their god of fire, worked at a hot forge to make weapons.	**Ex #1:** Vulcan's forge made sparks.
Ex #2: Our planet is made up of many layers of rock.	**Ex #2:** The top layers are the crust.	**Ex #2:** Deep beneath the crust is hot, molten magma.

Figure 5.17   Rubric for Writing Assignment

Only one or two complete sentences	Some complete sentences	Most of the sentences are complete.	All of the sentences are complete.
None or few of the sentences start with a capital letter and end with a period.	Some of the sentences start with a capital letter and end with a period.	Most of the sentences start with a capital letter and end with a period.	All the sentences start with a capital letter and end with a period.
Student identifies few of the main ideas.	Student identifies some of the main ideas.	Student identifies most of the main ideas.	Student identifies all the main ideas.
Student chooses textual evidence that fits only a few of the main ideas.	Student chooses textual evidence that fits some of the main ideas.	Student chooses textual evidence that fits most of the main ideas.	Student chooses textual evidence that fits all of the main ideas.

- *Lower-grade students work in pairs reading a book about volcanoes appropriate for their grade level. They identify key terms related to volcanoes, including words like lava, volcanic ash, gases, magma, and crust, and write a definition of each from the reading. They also can draw a picture of the layers of a volcanic mountain and label the layers.*

FOUND POEMS

Give pairs of students strips of paper and have them choose phrases and key words from their main ideas and textual evidence charts or the reading and write those words and phrases on their slips of paper. Have them put those strips in an order that makes sense to them to show what they know about volcanoes. Pass out poster paper and have students write their poems and illustrate them. Display the poems around the room and have students read their poems in pairs, in unison, or separately.

- *Lower-grade students work in their pairs to create a diamante poem about volcanoes. The lines to make up the diamond-shaped poem would include:*
  - Line 1: volcanoes
  - Line 2: two adjectives that describe volcanoes
  - Line 3: three verbs that describe volcanoes
  - Line 4: four nouns that describe volcanoes
  - Live 5: three more adjectives that describe volcanoes
  - Line 6: two more nouns that describe volcanoes
  - Line 7: repeat the word *volcanoes*

HISTORICAL FICTION: *THE DOG OF POMPEII*: FACT OR FICTION?

Have students read another anchor text from their basal reading program, *The Dog of Pompeii* by Louis Untermeyer. Next have them fill in a chart with details about characters and events in the story and indicate if each detail is fact or fiction. Then have them explain why they made their choice. Remind them to use sentences with words like *because* to tell why and provide a model sentence.

- *Lower-grade students can listen to a read-aloud narrative nonfiction or historical fiction piece about a natural disaster. Together, the teacher and the students list details of the story and decide if each detail is fact or fiction.*

WRITING AND PERFORMING A MYTH

Drawing on the myths about volcanoes presented in Seymour's book, *Volcanoes,* have students work in pairs to research a myth about a natural disaster. If students have roots in other countries, have them search for myths from that country. Each pair should choose a myth and write down the details to share with the rest of the class.

Figure 5.18   Fact or Fiction Chart

Detail about character or event	Fact? Or fiction?	Why?

Explain to students that that they will write a short play based on the myth they have researched about a natural disaster. The play should answer questions such as: "What might have caused it?" "Who might have caused it?" "What were the results?" Have students brainstorm ideas and then write a short play to illustrate their myth.

Show students the cover and the first few pages of a play. Ask the students to talk in small groups and make a list of what they notice about the differences between the way the myths they have researched are written and a play is written. Have students report back and lead a class discussion about the differences between the way myths and plays are written. Write students' ideas on the whiteboard. Have students add more differences as they read myths and write their plays. Have students perform their plays. They may bring costumes and props from home.

- *Students in lower grades can read different myths in groups about how and why volcanoes, floods, earthquakes, or other natural disasters occur. Have the students plan and act out their myths.*

EXPLORING THE SAN FRANCISCO EARTHQUAKE OF 1906

Show students pictures of earthquakes from the Internet or other sources and show a video about how earthquakes occur. Have students respond to the pictures and videos and encourage students to share personal stories of experiences with earthquakes.

Read students one of the many trade book stories about the 1906 San Francisco earthquake and ask them to write answers to questions such as the following:

1. Why did so many people come to live in San Francisco in the first place?
2. What causes earthquakes?
3. Did the people of San Francisco get any warnings before the big earthquake hit? What were they?
4. Why were so many buildings destroyed in that earthquake?
5. What are people doing today to be safer in the case of an earthquake?
6. Students can share answers in pairs and with the whole group.

IF I LIVED ON AN ICEBERG/GLACIER

Have students look at pictures of icebergs and glaciers. Based on the pictures, students finish the following sentences. Student sentences should rely on different senses and use conditional mood following the pattern *"If _____ I would _____."*

- If I lived on a glacier, what would I see?
- If I lived on a glacier, what would I hear?
- If I lived on a glacier, what activities would I do?

Read the anchor text *Icebergs and Glaciers* (Seymour, 2018). Have students use information from the book to add details to their sentences.

SEQUENCE CHART AND PARAGRAPH WRITING ACTIVITY FROM ANCHOR TEXT *ICEBERGS AND GLACIERS*

Give students a sequence chart (see Figure 5.19) and ask them to explain the steps in order of how a snowflake eventually can become an iceberg or a glacier using information from their anchor text *Icebergs and Glaciers* and the Internet. Have them draw each stage and then write below in the text boxes what happens during each step. After students complete the graphic individually, have them share their

Figure 5.19 Sequence Chart

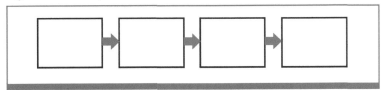

Figure 5.20 Checklist for Process Paragraph

Name: _____

Did I . . . ?	Yes	No
Indent the first line of the paragraph		
Begin with a topic sentence that introduces the steps		
Write complete sentences		
Connect the sentences with signal words showing time		
Write a concluding sentence that sums up the steps in the process		

answers with a partner, making changes as needed if they realize they did not complete their sequence chart correctly. Then, have them work individually to write a paragraph to explain the steps in the formation of an iceberg or a glacier. Remind them to use signal words showing the sequence to connect the sentences in their paragraph. Give students the checklist for a process paragraph (see Figure 5.20) to use as they write. They should turn in the checklist with their completed paragraphs.

- *Lower-grade students can watch a grade-level-appropriate video on glaciers. With the teacher, they can fill in the sequence chart about how glaciers are formed as a class. Afterwards, the students and the teacher can write about how glaciers are formed as a language experience activity with students dictating what happens using sequence words such as* first, second, third, next, *and* after that.

KWL CHARTING THE *TITANIC*

Before reading the anchor text, *Exploring the Titanic* (Ballard, 1988), have students brainstorm together what they already know and what they want to know about the *Titanic* and its sinking. Use this information to fill in the KW sections of the KWL chart (Figure 5.21).

Figure 5.21 KWL Chart: The *Titanic*

What do we know about the *Titanic*?	What do we want to know about the *Titanic*?	What have we learned about the *Titanic*?

- *Lower-grade students may or may not have background information on the* Titanic. *It is up to teachers to decide if they want to bring in this disaster. There are a few books and videos available for younger children. Most books are quite complex with much detail that may or may not be appropriate for lower grades. Teachers who do use the story can use the KWL chart, and if the story is historical fiction or narrative nonfiction, students can distinguish between fact and fiction.*

IDENTIFYING NARRATIVE AND FACTS IN NARRATIVE NONFICTION

Explain to the students that *Exploring the* Titanic is narrative nonfiction. In narrative nonfiction, the author uses elements of fiction including plot, setting, conflict, and character development but bases the narrative on facts from original source materials such as photographs, reliable accounts, and quotes from real people. From the reading, have students identify narrative elements including plot, setting, and conflict, and identify four characters telling about them and why they were on the *Titanic*. Have them use this information to fill out the narrative events chart (Figure 5.22).

Figure 5.22 **Narrative Events of the *Titanic***

Narrative		
Plot:	Setting:	Conflict:
Characters		
Character 1:	Character 2:	Character 3:	Character 4:

Next, have students choose five details about characters or events to decide whether each detail is fact or fiction, and then explain why it was fact or fiction. Have them use Figure 5.23 to record their answers.

Figure 5.23 **Fact or Fiction Chart: The *Titanic***

Detail about character or event	Fact? Or fiction?	Why?

After they complete their graphics, have students share their answers with a partner and explain each of their decisions. Next, lead the class in creating a master chart for the text, listing details of characters and events, labeling them as fact or fiction, and giving reasons for the decisions.

- *Students in lower grades can read a grade-level text about any natural disaster that is narrative nonfiction and identify what is fact and what is fiction.*

REVIEW ACTIVITIES FOR NATURAL DISASTERS UNIT

Writing Narrative Nonfiction About a Natural Disaster

Remind students that they have read different texts that are narrative nonfiction or historical fiction. Put students in their original *I Survived* groups and have the students create their own narrative nonfiction piece about the disaster they did for their posters or another natural disaster. Have them research source material on the disaster. They also need to create their own plot and characters for the narrative. The teacher evaluates the assignment with a checklist. Figure 5.24 shows a rating scale for this evaluation.

Figure 5.24   Rating Scale for Narrative Nonfiction

Name: _____

How well did the student . . . ?	Needs Work	Fair	Good	Excellent
Explain the plot				
Describe the setting				
Describe the characters				
Include an orientation				
Put the events in sequence				
Include a conclusion				

- *Students in lower grades: Students will read a grade level text that is narrative nonfiction and identify what is fact and what is fiction. They can also plan and act out the narrative nonfiction text.*

SIERRA: A POEM DEMONSTRATING PERSONIFICATION AND METAPHOR

Remind the students about the kinds of figurative language they have studied before including metaphor, simile, and personification. Remind them that personification is a type of figurative language that gives human qualities to nonhuman things.

Read together as a class the anchor poem *Sierra* and have students underline portions of the poem showing how the forces of nature change the mountain. Also, discuss how the author uses personification in describing the natural forces that have affected the mountain.

After reading the poem and identifying the examples of personification, have students choose a partner and write their own poems using personification. They are to choose a geographical feature (like the ocean, a river, a volcano, a rain forest, a lake), or a natural disaster (like an earthquake, a tornado, a blizzard, a drought, or a tsunami) and write a poem using personification. Have students create an illustrated poster with their poems. Have them read their poems to the class and then display their posters.

- *Students in lower grades can read any of a variety of poems about nature and write their own poems using descriptive language and rhyme.*

BASAL ANCHOR BOOKS FOR THE UNIT

Ballard, R. (1988). *Exploring the Titanic*. New York, NY: Scholastic.

Karwoski, G. L. (2006). *Quake! Disaster in San Francisco, 1906*. Atlanta, GA: Peachtree.

Seymour, S. (2006). *Volcanoes*. New York, NY: HarperCollins.

Seymour, S. (2018). *Icebergs and glaciers*. New York, NY: HarperCollins.

Siebert, D. (1996). *Sierra*. New York, NY: HarperCollins.

Untermeyer, L. (1932). *The dog of Pompeii*. In L. Untermeyer (Ed.), *The donkey of God*. New York, NY: Harcourt Brace.

BOOKS FOR LOWER GRADES IN BASAL TEXTS

Goodman, S., & Doolittle, M. (2006). *Life on ice*. Minneapolis, MN: Lerner.

Seymour, S. (2002). *Super storms*. San Francisco, CA: Chronicle Books.

SUPPLEMENTAL READINGS ON NATURAL DISASTERS IN ENGLISH AND SPANISH

Armour, C. (2012). *¡Terremotos!* Huntington Beach, CA: Teacher Created Materials.

Cosgrove, B. (2016). *Discover the world's weather from heat waves and droughts to blizzards and floods*. New York, NY: DK.

Dubowski, M. (2015). Titanic: *The disaster that shocked the world!* New York, NY: DK.

Feely, J. (2012). *Under the ice*. Temecula, CA: Okapi.

Feely, J. (2015). *Bajo el hielo*. Temecula, CA: Okapi.

Fullman, J. (2016). *The story of* Titanic *for children*. London, England: Carlton Kids.

Furgang, K. (2013). *National Geographic Kids: Everything volcanoes and earthquakes*. Washington, DC: National Geographic Children's Books.

Gregory, J., & Serra, S. (2017). *National Geographic Kids: If you were a kid aboard the* Titanic. New York, NY: C. Press/F. Watts Trade.

Griffey, H. (2010). *Earthquakes and other natural disasters*. New York, NY: DK.

Karwoski, G. L. (2006). *Quake! Disaster in San Francisco, 1906*. Atlanta, GA, Peachtree.

Kehret, P. (2015). *Escaping the great wave*. New York, NY: Simon and Schuster.

Kostigen, T. (2014). *Extreme weather: Surviving tornadoes, sandstorms, hailstorms, blizzards, and more*. Washington, DC: National Geographic Children's Books.

Love, D. (2011). *The glaciers are melting!* Mt. Pleasant, SC: Arbondale.

May, M. (2018a). *Nuestra tierra activa*. Temecula, CA: Okapi.

May, M. (2018b). *Our active earth*. Temecula, CA: Okapi.

Ohlin, N. (2016). *The* Titanic. New York, NY: Little Bee Books.

Rice, W. B. (2010*). Los volcanes*. Huntington Beach, CA: Teacher Created Materials.

Shanahan, K. (2012a). *Forest fires*. Temecula, CA: Okapi.

Shanahan, K. (2012b). *Living near a volcano*. Temecula, CA: Okapi.

Shanahan, K. (2015). *Vivir cerca de un volcán*. Temecula, CA: Okapi.

Stiefei, C. (2009). *Tsunamis*. New York, NY: Scholastic.

Tarshis, L. (2010*). I survived the sinking of the Titanic, 1912*. New York, NY: Scholastic.

Tarshis, L. (2011). *I survived Hurricane Katrina, 2005*. New York, NY: Scholastic.

Tarshis, L. (2013). *I survived the Japanese tsunami, 2011*. New York, NY: Scholastic.

Tarshis, L. (2014*). I survived the destruction of Pompeii, AD 79*. New York, NY: Scholastic.

Tarshis, L. (2015). *I survived the Great Chicago Fire, 1871*. New York, NY: Scholastic.

Tarshis, L. (2016a). *I survived the eruption of Mount St. Helens, 1980*. New York, NY: Scholastic.

Tarshis, L. (2016b*). I survived: True stories of extreme weather*. New York, NY: Scholastic.

Tarshis, L. (2017). *Tornado terror: True tornado survival stories and amazing facts from history and today*. New York, NY: Scholastic.

Tarshis, L., and Dawson, S. (2012). *I survived the San Francisco earthquake, 1906*. New York, NY: Scholastic.

Watts, C., & Day, T. (2015). *Natural disasters: Confront the awesome power of nature from earthquakes and tsunamis to hurricanes*. New York, NY: DK.

Yep, L. (2008). *The earth dragon awakes: The San Franciso earthquake of 1906*. New York, NY: HarperCollins.

Yolen, J. (2003). *Color me a rhyme: Nature poems for young people*. Honesdale, PA: WordSong.

Professional References

Anderson, R., & Nagy, W. (1992). The vocabulary conundrum. *American Educator,* (Winter), *16*(4) 14–18, 44–47.

Chambliss, M. J., & Calfee, R. C. (1998). *Textbooks for learning: Nurturing children's minds.* Maiden, MA: Blackwell.

Creese, A., & Blackledge, A. (2010). Translanguaging in the bilingual classroom: A pedagogy for learning and teaching? *Modern Language Journal, 94*(1), 103–115.

Cummins, J. (2000). *Language, power and pedagogy: Bilingual children in the crossfire.* Tonawanda, NY: Multilingual Matters.

Cummins, J. (2007). Rethinking monolingual instructional strategies in multilingual classrooms. *Canadian Journal of Applied Linguistics, 10*(2), 221–240.

Cummins, J. (2008). BICS and CALP: Empirical and theoretical status of the distinction. In N. Hornberger (Ed.), *Encyclopedia of Language and Education* (2nd ed., Vol. 2, pp. 71–84). New York, NY: Springer Science and Business Media LLC.

Dewitz, P., & Jones, J. (2012). Using basal readers: From dutiful fidelity to intelligent decision making. *The Reading Teacher, 66*(6), 301–400.

Dewitz, P., Jones, J., & Leahy, S. (2009). Comprehension strategy instruction in core reading programs. *Reading Research Quarterly, 44*(2), 102–126.

Dewitz, P., Leahy, S., & Jones, J. (2010). *The essential guide to selecting and using core reading programs.* Newark, NJ: International Reading Association.

Ebe, A. (2011). Culturally relevant books: Bridges to reading engagement for English language learners. *Insights on Learning Disabilities, 8*(2), 31–45.

Freeman, D. E., & Freeman, Y. S. (1999). The California reading initiative: A formula for failure for bilingual students? *Language Arts, 76*(3), 241–248.

Freeman, D., & Freeman, Y. (2011). *Between worlds: Access to second language acquisition* (3rd ed.). Portsmouth, NH: Heinemann.

Freeman, Y. (1988a). The contemporary Spanish basal reader in the United States: How does it reflect current understanding of the reading process? *NABE Journal, 13*(1), 59–74.

Freeman, Y. (1988b). Do Spanish methods and materials reflect current understanding of the reading process? *The Reading Teacher, 41*(7), 654–664.

Freeman, Y. S., & Freeman, D. E. (1992). *Whole language for second language learners.* Portsmouth, NH: Heinemann.

Fu, D., Hadjioannou, X., & Zhou, X. (2019). *Translanguaging for emergent bilinguals: Inclusive teaching in the linguistically diverse classroom.* New York, NY: Teachers College Press.

García, O. (2009). *Bilingual education in the 21st century: A global perspective.* Malden, MA: Wiley-Blackwell.

García, O., Johnson, S. I., & Seltzer, K. (2017). *The translanguaging classroom.* Philadelphia, PA: Caslon.

Goodman, K., Shannon, P., Freeman, Y., & Murphy, S. (1988). *Report card on basal readers.* New York, NY: Richard C. Owen.

Guthrie, J. (2004). Teaching for literacy engagement. *Journal of Literacy Research, 36*(1), 1–29.

Krashen, S. (1982). *Principles and practice in second language acquisition.* New York, NY: Pergamon.

Marzano, R. (2004). *Building background knowledge for academic achievement: Research on what works in schools.* Alexandria, VA: Association for Supervision and Curriculum Development.

Marzano, R., Pickering, D., & Pollock, J. (2001). *Classroom instruction that works: Research-based strategies for increasing student achievement.* Alexandria, VA: Association for Curriculum Development and Supervision.

MacDonald, R., Boals, T., Castro, M., Cook, G., Lundberg, T., & White, P. (2015). *Formative language assessment for English learners.* Portsmouth, NH: Heinemann.

McKeown, M. G., Beck, I. L., & Blake, R. G. K. (2009). Rethinking reading comprehension instruction: A comparison of instruction for strategies and content approaches. *Reading Research Quarterly, 44*(4), 218–253.

Pally, M. (Ed.) (2000). *Sustained content teaching in academic ESL/EFL: A practical approach.* Boston, MA: Houghton Mifflin.

Paulson, E., & Freeman, A. (2003). *Insight from the eyes: The science of effective reading instruction.* Portsmouth, NH: Heinemann.

Rog, L., & Burton, W. (2001–2). Matching texts and readers: Leveling early reading materials for assessment and instruction. *Reading Teacher, 55*(4), 348–356.

Schmoker, M. (2019). The problem with literacy programs. *Education Week, 38*(24), 18.

Shanahan, T. (2016). How can you support basal readers when we know it's teachers that matter? [blog post]. *Reading Rockets.*

U.S. Department of Education, OELA (2016). *Non-regulatory guidance: English learners and Title III of the Elementary and Secondary Education Act (ESEA), as amended by the Every Student Succeeds Act (ESSA).* Washington, DC: Office of English Language Acquisition.

Walsh, K. (2003). Basal readers: The lost opportunity to build the knowledge that Propels comprehension. *American Educator, 27*(1), 24–27.

Index

A SAGE Publishing Company

Helping educators make the greatest impact

CORWIN HAS ONE MISSION: to enhance education through intentional professional learning.

We build long-term relationships with our authors, educators, clients, and associations who partner with us to develop and continuously improve the best evidence-based practices that establish and support lifelong learning.

Solutions YOU WANT | Experts YOU TRUST | Results YOU NEED

EVENTS

>>> **INSTITUTES**
Corwin Institutes provide large regional events where educators collaborate with peers and learn from industry experts. Prepare to be recharged and motivated!

corwin.com/institutes

ON-SITE PD

>>> **ON-SITE PROFESSIONAL LEARNING**
Corwin on-site PD is delivered through high-energy keynotes, practical workshops, and custom coaching services designed to support knowledge development and implementation.

corwin.com/pd

>>> **PROFESSIONAL DEVELOPMENT RESOURCE CENTER**
The PD Resource Center provides school and district PD facilitators with the tools and resources needed to deliver effective PD.

corwin.com/pdrc

ONLINE

>>> **ADVANCE**
Designed for K–12 teachers, Advance offers a range of online learning options that can qualify for graduate-level credit and apply toward license renewal.

corwin.com/advance

Contact a PD Advisor at (800) 831-6640 or visit www.corwin.com for more information